Immortal Jaguar

HUGH FOX

© Hugh Fox 2011

First published in Great Britain in 2011 by Skylight Press,
210 Brooklyn Road, Cheltenham, Glos GL51 8EA

All rights reserved. Except for the quotation of short passages for the purposes of criticism and review, no part of this publication may be reproduced, stored in a retrieval system or transmitted, in any form or by any means, electronic, mechanical, photocopying, recording or otherwise, without the prior consent of the copyright holder and publisher.

Hugh Fox has asserted his right to be identified as the author of this work.

Illustrations by Maria Bernadete Costa-Fox
Designed and typeset by Rebsie Fairholm
Printed and bound in Great Britain by Lightning Source, Milton Keynes

www.skylightpress.co.uk

ISBN 978-1-908011-09-1

Immortal Jaguar

IMMORTAL JAGUAR

I first heard about the immortals on my first trip to Peru back in June of 1958. A year earlier I had married the Peruvian writer, Lucia Ungaro Zevallos while I was a graduate student at the University of Illinois, but none of the family, except Lucia's brother, Mario (an M.D. who was in the middle of a residency in pathology at St. Luke's in Chicago) had been able to attend the wedding and so the June 1958 trip was essentially my first encounter with the whole family. Lucia's mother lived in Lima and we stayed with her for about a month, but July in Lima is in the middle of the winter and it is extremely damp and cold and everyone is walking around with head colds and flu and my mother-in-law suggested that we go and visit her dead husband's brother, Lucia's uncle, in Antisuyo: "*Realmente no tienen estaciones alli. Y el esta muy amigo con Lucia. Vivió aca en Lima cuando ella era niña.* There really aren't any seasons there. He is a good friend of Lucia's. He used to live here in Lima when she was a child."

So we took a plane to Cuzco and from there went by bus to the Urubamba Valley and down into the edge of the Madre De Dios jungle.

It is an area that the Peruvian government is trying to re-develop. I say "re-develop" because in ancient times the population there was quite dense, although it wasn't abandoned because of the Spanish conquest in the sixteenth century, but seems actually to have been abandoned much earlier. Some commentators like Padre Ricardo de Cobo, who worked with Indians in the area on the eastern side of the Andes and who collected oral history and folklore in the Arapacho area, claim that according to Indian traditions the area was abandoned as far back as the eighth century. I was able to obtain a photocopy of De Cobo's *Historia de Antisuyo* through the inter-library loan system at the John Carter Brown Library at Brown University (where I had a John Carter Brown Library grant in the mid-1960s) and I found the following account of the Madre de Dios area:

> ... *los indios Arapachos tienen fabulas extravagantes sobre la historia (mejor dicho "pre-historia," porque estamos en las epocas de la pura lejenda) de la región al lado de la selva de Madre de Dios. Dicen que Ilegaran alli los gigantes despues del Deluvio y los immortales que vivian alli antes huyeron de sus hogares y se refugiaran en cavernas cuyos entradas entaban desconocidos por todos. Me dijeron con todo seriedad que "Los immortales aindo estan por alli,*

pero nadie atreve acercar este area porque son hechiceros y pueden despertar los malos espiritus que te entran y acaban con Usted desde adentro. Es un tipo de maldición sino sin palabras, utilizando signos diabolicos." Lo interesante para me fue la mezcla de historias biblicas y locales, la referencia al Deluvio, por ejemplo, y ate los gigantes que estan mencionados en Genesis VI, verso 4 con el nombre en Hebreo de Nephilim. El nombre en Arapacho es Napiliam que solamente yo puedo explicar (1.) Por coincidencia, o (2.) La posibilidad de que uno de los tribus perdidos de los Judeos Ilegaran en estes partes en tempos remotos.
(Sevilla: Privately Printed, 1643, III, pp.22-23)

... the Arapachos Indians have extravagant fables about the history (or more accurately 'pre-history', because we are in the times of pure legend) of the area on the edge of the Madre de Dios jungle. They say that giants arrived there after the Flood and that the immortals that lived there before fled from their homes and took refuge in caverns/caves with entrances that were unknown to everyone. They told me with total seriousness that "The Immortals are still there, but nobody dares go near this area because they [i.e. the Immortals] are sorcerers and they are able to awaken evil spirits that enter into you and destroy you from inside. It is a type of curse but without words, using diabolical signs." What is interesting to me is the mixture of biblical and local history and, for example, the mention of the Flood and even of the giants which are mentioned in Genesis, Chapter VI, Verse 4, where the giants are referred to as Nephilim. The name in Arapacho is Napilam, which I can explain only (1.) by coincidence or (2.) the possibility that one of the lost tribes of the Jews arrived in these parts in remote times.
(My translation)

These links between the ancient Middle East and the New World were noticed by many of the early Spanish historians and ethnologists (most, of them, of course, priests, many of whom read some Hebrew) like Fray Diego de Duran, B. de Sahagun, etc and when they saw the statues of the chief pre-Inca god in the Andes, Viracocha Kon-Tiki, many of them compared the statues to St. Bartholomew. Diego de Duran, for example, in his *Book of the Gods and Rites* noticed detailed similarities between Aztec rituals and the ancient Jewish rituals described in Leviticus. So De Cobo's observations were far from unusual.

The one thing that sets them apart from other accounts is his mention of "immortals." As far as I can determine he is the only writer to have written about the Madre de Dios area (and specifically the Arapachos) in post-Conquest times. Most of the other writers concerning themselves with the much more visible and accessible Incas – which, of course, may account for the uniqueness of his account.

I am getting ahead of my story here, though. I obtained De Cobo's *Historia* after I had returned from my visit to Lucia's uncle's *hacienda* in the Madre de Dios jungle, not before, and the interesting thing for me was that a sixteenth century source agreed with what I had just heard (as oral history/folklore) from the mouth of Lucia's uncle himself.

Lucia's uncle, Mario, owned huge tracts of land in an area that had been in her family since the sixteenth century and which had finally come into his possession (because of deaths, very complicated patterns of wills and inheritances) some fifteen years earlier.

Certainly Lucia's mother, Henrietta, was 100% correct when she said there really were no "seasons" in the area, except perhaps for a short rainy season which, fortunately for us, had just ended. It wasn't quite jungle, still up a few thousand feet and the climate reminded me a little of Mexico City and/or Caracas. In fact it was the closest that I had ever come to heaven on earth. It was like Quito in a way, but didn't have Quito's punishing height, similar to La Paz and the Bolivian *altiplano* in its briskness, but, again, without the strain of altitudes above ten or twelve thousand feet.

Even fifty years ago I always had difficulty with extreme altitudes, but here on Uncle Mario's *hacienda* everything seemed to be just right – except for the bugs ... and the bats.

We would have dinner in a huge dining room that was totally open, a massive table under a wrought iron candelabrum filled with (I counted them) 18 candles.

Candles on the table. No electric light.

"I don't believe in 'artificiality' out here. I accept things for what they are. In fact I welcome what most people call 'the primitive.' For me it's not 'primitive,' but the natural order of things. After you live here for a while, you'll see, you go back to 'their' cities and you see 'them' – and not us – as the 'primitives.'"

Only the jungle that surrounded us was filled with bats. Insects would be attracted by the candles and the bats would fly in after them so there was always an insect hum in the background accompanied by the quick in and out flights of the bats that were so quick, in fact, that the first night I almost thought I was imagining them.

And I must have very strange ears, because the others could barely hear the so-called supersonic screams of the bats themselves. *But I could hear them.* Uncle Mario said it was my imagination, but it wasn't. For me the whole room was crisscrossed with radar beeps that no one else but me (and the bats) could hear.

Lots of fried yucca root which was a kind of fibrous, rough almost-potato. Lots of pork (they kept pigs), fried bananas, home-made rum.

"It's so wonderful to have you both here. Stay a year. Two years. Whatever," Uncle Mario said, turning to me, and then Lucia. "I have such wonderful memories of this little girl – when she was a little girl. She's turned out to be quite a woman. She still writes, I suppose …"

"Of course," said Lucia.

"I remember my brother, Sebastián, he was a mining engineer in the mountains. He'd come into Lima to see the family and Lucia would always have another book of poetry written. When did you get your first book of poetry published?"

"I was eight," she said, "of course, looking back, it seems 'infantile' now, but in those days …"

"In those days!" said Uncle Mario, sitting back, taking a long, slow drink of rum, letting 'those days' slide through his mind …

"I can just imagine what you're thinking," said Lucia, "images of beaches, ice cream, the Indians with their little 'horse-boats,' *camarones* [shrimp] … all the family gathered together …."

"See, you're a mind-reader!" laughed Mario as one of the Indian servants brought in a big platter of freshly cut pineapple, a very old woman, tiny, as dark as teakwood, strangely oriental, *ensimismado*, as they say, which is difficult to translate, something like 'folded in on herself' … meditative … I might even say Zen-like.

"Now if you could read Doña Teresa's mind," directing his attention to the old Indian who at the same time was very aware of everything around her and, paradoxically, totally cut off, in her own world, so to speak, "that's a mind to read. Some things very inspiring. Some things terrifying. Some of the most incredible things I've ever heard … but, somehow, I still believe them … she's not from around here but from the other side of the mountains, Antisuyo … isn't that right Doña Teresa?"

"*El Señor sabe*," said the old Indian, "The Master knows."

And you notice I translate *señor* as "master" because that it is the connotation that it carried with it in those days.

He asked the old Indian, "May I tell my niece and her husband everything you told me about the 'ancients'?"

And again the same answer, coming across huge distances from inside her. As if she were totally (again "Zen-like") detached from us, the night, the bats, her 'station' in life, totally her own interiorised person.

"*El Señor sabe.*" "The Master knows."

"*Bueno,*" said Uncle Mario, sitting back, Doña Teresa having placed the pineapple on the table slowly dissolving into the shadows and out into the darkness, Uncle Mario offering me a cigar out of a little carved wooden box on the table next to his plate. Which I accepted. Sweet, aromatic tobacco. I looked at the box for a moment, a jaguar carved on the cover, standing on its hind feet, with a human head in its front paws. Reminiscent of some of the statues at San Agustín in Colombia. Of course I knew what it meant. The jaguar was the spirit-helper from the Other World who had come to destroy the Old Self of someone who had just taken a dose of some sacred hallucinogen – part of the process of death and rebirth associated with shamanistic transitions into higher states of being.

"Do you like it?" asked Uncle Mario.

"Well made. Interesting," I answered.

"I give it to you," he said, then sat back, inhaling deeply on the cigar, reminding me of the cigars used in Macumba in Bahia, Brazil, tobacco itself becoming a sacred drug that brought the user into the Spirit-World. Uncle Mario put his head back, closed his eyes and started to talk. And it wasn't as if he himself were talking but The Spirits were talking *through* him, as if he himself had slowly and purposefully allowed himself to become an instrument for the Spirits from the Nether World to communicate through.

Lucia was very uncomfortable. Her beloved uncle was no longer just her beloved uncle but some sort of "conduit" for truths from Other Worlds. And, to be honest, I was just as uncomfortable as she was, if not more so. I was just at the beginning of the studies that were to occupy me for the next forty years, but even then I had a healthy fear of the realities that lay waiting on the other side of the invisible barrier that separates us from the Spirit World.

"Doña Teresa has talked to me for many hours. At times like this. At night, when there is no one else around, my wife in Trujillo visiting her family, the kids with her, going to school, as I suppose they must… and Teresa has told me many things that conflict with everything that I am 'supposed' to believe – *que debo creer* – but which have nothing to do with what I really believe – *lo que realmente creo*. You know all the old prayers – I BELIEVE IN GOD, THE FATHER ALMIGHTY AND IN JESUS CHRIST, HIS ONLY BEGOTTEN SON … you know how it all goes … the trinity … the incarnation … only what if I were to tell you Doña Teresa's Credo: I BELIEVE IN THE GODS WHO DESCENDED FROM

THE SUN AND WHO TOOK ON HUMAN FORM AND LIVED IN THE SACRED CENTRE AT THE CENTRE OF THE WORLD AND WHO LIVE FOREVER NOW IN THE SACRED CAVES WHERE THEY HAVE TAKEN REFUGE FROM THE SATANIC GIANTS OF EVIL."

Uncle Mario opening his eyes, sitting back up to the table, throwing his cigar on the floor and squashing it out with the heel of his boot.

"Well, that's enough tonight maybe. You probably think I'm crazy, don't you? Too much sacred cactus, too much *coca*, too much *ayahuasca* … but let me tell you something, Dante's *Comedia Divina* is nothing compared to the Reality that surrounds us here … nothing …"

Lucia was obviously relieved. What she had just got a sample of was a side to Uncle Mario's personality that she really didn't want to explore.

It was our second night at the *hacienda* and she was very much of a city person, not at all interested in explorations of the Spirit World, a Ph.D. in Romance Languages from the University of Illinois, very academic, very on track in terms of the rational, 'normal' world, very much turned off to the occult, 'irrational,' let's call it the obverse side of reality.

"I'm so tired. The rum, I guess. And all that food. I love the yucca." Getting up, yawning, going into the main part of the house where the bedrooms were. We slept surrounded by mosquito netting, of course, with a spiral of some sort of mosquito repellent, burning like incense in the room all night long.

I waited, let her go, and just as Mario was about to follow her, I stopped him.

"Could I ask you a question?"

"Of course," he answered, sitting back down, "anything …" lighting up another cigar, pouring himself a little more rum, offering some to me. Which I accepted. He wasn't in any hurry. Lucia could take care of herself. He obviously had much more he *wanted* to say but had been reluctant to say as long as she was still there.

"OK … there's this ancient Sumerian poem, *Gilgamesh*, about a voyage across the ocean to ANAKU, the Tin-Lands … which I see as a reference to what are now the ancient ruins of TIAWANAKU in Bolivia, right in the middle of the Bolivian tin country … I mean I'm talking about a poem from what is today Iraq that dates back to at least 3,000 B.C. …"

Uncle Mario unfazed, not suprised, as if this were part of the lore which he already knew but which usually – when I sprang it on anyone in the academic world – was always met with disbelief and even anger.

"And the question?" he asked, smiling, "You still haven't asked it."

"Bear with me," I said feeling strangely uncomfortable with the man, as if he already knew what I was going to ask, "when Gilgamesh and his friend Enkidu finally get to Anaku, Enkidu dies and Gilgamesh dives into a lake in order to get some 'thorn-apples' *[manzanas espinosas]* which are said to – and this is exactly the text – 'make old men young again' *['hacen los viejos jovenes de nuevo']* … some sort of 'youth-apples,' I don't know …"

"Of course you don't know. What do you think, that so-called 'civilisation' progresses in some sort of straight line? I'm an engineer by profession. This whole *hacienda*-business in a sense was thrust on me by circumstances. I'm not complaining, I'm a wealthy man, and I'll be wealthier still once they get real roads and railways into this area and we can really can get the fruit out. But I see 'civilisation' as something going in reverse. There was a time, call it the Golden Age, when Man really was in touch with the 'forces' of nature. That whole picture of the Garden of Eden. Adam talks to the animals, has control over everything, no aging, no death. It all comes *after* the Fall … but… I see myself as a religious man, but I think the story of Adam and the Garden of Eden happened exactly the opposite of the way it is told in the bible. You remember how Eve gets Adam to eat one of the apples of the Tree of Good and Evil and that brings Evil and Death into the world. In reality it was exactly the opposite. Eve gets Adam to eat the apple and it makes him immortal."

Uncle Mario sat back smiling, a little drunk, a little debauched looking, a little too heavy, too much easy living. He never had to move a finger. It was all done for him by his army of Indians out there working the *hacienda* for him.

But I felt that I almost had my hands on the elusive truth about the Fall of Man, the Before and After of mankind's happiness since the Creation or – in more 'modern' terms – since man had evolved from whatever he had evolved from. There had been a time, though, hadn't there, before The Fall, when not only had Man been totally in sync with the world around him, but death was unknown … or …

"Do you really believe there was a time when people didn't die?" I asked.

He stopped smoking, threw his second cigar down on the floor and recorked the bottle of rum, finished off the glass he had in his hand. One last swallow, something fatalistic and resigned in the way he put down the glass and stared at me, stared and stared until I didn't know what to expect, some sort of fit, madness, actually began to feel uneasy, almost afraid, a huge knife hanging, as always, from his rough leather belt. Were there things about Uncle Mario that I didn't know, shouldn't, didn't want to know?

He sat there staring at me for, who knows, half an hour. Then a drop of hot wax fell from the overhead candelabrum on to his hand and he winced in pain, ("*Carajo!* Son of a bitch!") wiped the wax off with a handkerchief he pulled out of his pocket, smiled a smile that was practically a snarl.

"You're a big specialist in myths and all this stuff, right? That's what my niece, Lucia, tells me … OK … let me put you to a test. How many candles are in that candelabrum?"

I looked up. I'd already counted them when I'd first got there.

"Eighteen."

"Now why would I have the local blacksmith *ferrero* make me a massive thing like that with eighteen, not nineteen, not twenty, candles in it?"

"Well," I started to answer, "in Maya *uinac* is man and *uinal* is year, and the Mayas begin the year-count with the number of the fingers and toes, twenty. And you multiply twenty by eighteen to get a three hundred and sixty day solar year …"

Uncle Mario laughed a sneering, snarling laugh and got up out of his chair.

"Professors! You see what they know! Who am I to have eighteen candles hanging over my dinner table every night? Am I a Maya or something? What does *ui-whatever* have to do with me? Nothing … maybe there are things that Lucia hasn't told you about herself, about the family, but let me say this, if anyone has the right to say it, I do – the Rabbis in Genesis misrepresented the ancient truths about The Fall. You don't really think there is one God do you? Shema Israel … Echod … *one*? Maybe that's why I'm out here in the middle of the high jungle and not in Trujillo or Lima – so I can believe what I believe, worship what I worship. How old do you think I am?"

"I don't know. Fifty?"

"I am Lucia's father's older brother and he was seventy when he died ten years ago!" Mario's voice down to a whisper now, as if he didn't want the Night itself to hear.

Then stopping, opening the little carved box with the jaguar with the human head in its hands, taking out all the cigars but one, and handing it to me, "here, I said it's yours, it's yours! And goodnight, my friend …" coming over and giving me an embrace that almost hurt, it was that powerful.

And out he walked. Or perhaps I should stay 'stalked,' 'loped,' like a wolf, a jaguar, not like a man at all. Certainly not a very, very *old* man.

I sat back down, looked up staring at the candelabrum, trying to figure out what special significance the number eighteen might have for him. And then it hit me. Of course. Why should he know Hebrew? Somewhere deep inside me I had a few half forgotten facts that suddenly got activated. I'd spent most of my life in the library or in class, was Jesuit-educated, which had really given me my whole thrust into ancient myths and religions – and one of my best friends in New York (where I usually worked two months of the year on *The Smith* as an editor-writer) was the great kabbalistic scholar, Menke Katz. You'd go to his house for dinner and spend eight hours listening to arcane Jewish lore. The man was the world's greatest scholar in obscure little facts in ancient Jewish mysticism that no one else knew anything about – or even *wanted* to know. In Hebrew every letter also has a number value, and if you take the two letters that make up the word for Life (CH-AI) they add up to eighteen. So essentially the number eighteen was a code-number for Life itself. In fact this whole 18=Life business wasn't just Jewish but went back to neolithic times. You'd find stalactites in caves rounded off to resemble breasts with eighteen red (ochre) dots around them. All sorts of associations here – milk, blood, life, eighteen ...

One thing I'd learned from Katz was that Jewish lore often incorporated into it facts and theories, ideas, myths, beliefs from very, very ancient times.

So what Uncle Mario was telling me, wasn't he, was that he was a Jew, that under the Catholic façade his Jewishness was still there, probably going back to the times of the Spanish Inquisition when you had a choice – either convert to Catholicism or die. So Jews "converted," but not entirely, oftentimes never lost a hidden, subterranean current of Jewishness in their lives.

In a way it was like the Indians themselves, Catholic on the surface, but under the surface, the Old Religion was still alive and well. In Maud Oakes' *The Two Crosses of Todos Santos* she talks about the two crosses they had in Todos Santos in Guatemala – one Christian, the other pre-Christian, The Cross of the Four Directions, the symbol of the ancient sun-religion.

I must have been sitting there spacey and floating, under the guttering candles for half an hour thinking about these things, thinking that, really, I ought to take notes as was my custom, keep a diary, get it all down on paper, when suddenly the old Indian woman who had been there before, Doña Teresa, came into the dining room and startled me.

And why shouldn't I be startled? Who knew what was out there in the darkness? Jaguars, leopards, huge snakes. I almost jumped out of my skin when she suddenly appeared out of the darkness and walked into the flicking light cast by the candles.

"*Disculpame, señor*, I didn't mean to frighten you, I've come to clean things up," she said. "Could I offer you a little herbal tea, to help you sleep?"

"Why not," I answered.

She went to the far end of the dining hall to where the ovens were and in a few moments came back with an old teapot and a cup, obviously imported, probably from Spain. The designs on both the teapot and cup had a Spanish Baroque-Rococo look about them, all curlicues and lotus-like tendrils. It had probably been brought from Spain hundreds of years earlier. The whole country, especially in out of the way backwaters like this, was a giant antique shop. Or maybe even a little more than "antique." That's too superficial and easy – but call it an antiquities shop. Because lots of the culture here obviously went back thousands and thousands of years; although even I, at that time, had no idea just how far.

"Thanks a lot," I said and poured myself a cup of tea, slowly started sipping on it, as Doña Teresa started to sweep up with a very primitive broom of obviously local manufacture.

"Do you like it?" she asked.

"Yes, yes," I said. A strange bitter, acrid taste to the tea. And an undertaste, almost as if it had been smoked. All kinds of strange associations flitted through my head – marijuana back in San Francisco, horehound coughdrops, smoked herring, grape leaves. It was a totally new taste for me, but obviously linked with other compounds from my distant past.

I'd always been a little leery of drugs. My father was an M.D. who was a legal supplier of morphine to registered addicts and when I was a kid we lived in an apartment right next to his office and I'd play in the waiting room, talk to all kinds of addicts, who always said the same thing: "Keep away from this stuff, once it gets its jaws into you, it never lets go." I smoked a little grass during my hippy years in San Francisco, but adamantly had refused (as an anthropologist) ever to take hallucinogenic drugs of any sort. Then I started thinking about the Sumerian story of *Gilgamesh* and the thorn-apples of immortality. What was that all about, really? Just mythological nonsense or ... ? Funny associations to be running through my head. Or were they?

Doña Teresa finished sweeping up and came over to where I was sitting, turned a chair around to face me and sat down, obviously exhausted.

"I'm getting old," she said.

I wanted to ask her *how* old, but...

"So you're not from around here, then?"

"No, I'm from…" lifting her hand and waving it toward the northwest, "*mas alla.*"

Which meant both "more that way" and "the world beyond." She got up and brought a cup back for herself. "If it doesn't bother the Master, we can drink a little tea together."

"On the contrary … it's a pleasure …"

"Many people think that I'm just an ignorant old lady," she started to say, sipping at her tea, "as if all the answers came from … you know … what would you call it … *los perritos* – the 'specialists' … the people who know … only what do they know? What they know, or what they *knew*?" as she continued talking, her voice changing, from the thin, watery voice of an old lady into something much more guttural, changing in register, soprano, mezzo soprano, alto, tenor, bass, until it wasn't a voice any more, but more like a growl, and the growl itself growing more sonorous, fuller, more hollow, as if she were speaking out of the heart of some cavern deep inside her. "They think I am merely some ignorant old woman, Indian, 'the Indians' always with contempt … but what are we, really, but the Elder Race, we who have seen the gods becoming gods ourselves…" her face starting to change, the sagging old face slowly becoming taut, the eyes and mouth becoming more feline, and her body, as if it were growing, her fingers shortening, rounding out and becoming more clawlike, standing up now, towering over me, what was she ten, twelve feet tall, suddenly all pretence gone, all attempts to cloak what she really was under the melting-away flesh of a harmless old lady, no more words now but only resonant growls, and it was as if I could still understand what she was saying, although she wasn't really 'saying' anything.

"From the first I knew you were 'different,' you had the special aura about you, the air danced around you, spots of light in the air. You came in a serpent boat from the Past looking like the Master of Animals. And the minute I saw you I decided to take you in to become one of us. Only first you must die. Death is the first step of the Great Purification. You must go to the centre of the world and die and only then, a child again, with the year itself slashed across your chest, can I hold you in my arms and offer you to the old-man-become-new-again sun …" in a sudden instant stepping behind me and wrapping her paws around my neck, pushing my head forward so (I imagined, still thinking of everything in very precise, scientific, occidental terms) the carotid arteries would hang down and not be protected lying along the sides of the trachea. I remembered, during my first year of Medicine at the Stritch School of Medicine in Chicago, our anatomy professor, in one particularly sick remark, telling us "In case anyone here wants to commit suicide by slitting their throat, be sure to lean forward so you let the carotid arteries hang loose ..." Ha, ha, ha, ha ... in my mind memories of Professor Nelson's belly-laughs somehow twinning together with the jaguar-woman's growls, like two twisted-together vines, as she lifted me up now and threw me backwards against the table, my head hanging off the edge, roaring at me "Do not be afraid, there cannot be resurrection without destruction, rebirth without death," lifting her enormous right paw, the claws enormous, curved shining knives, ripping my neck open, not needing to worry about the carotid arteries flattening against the trachea, ripping open the trachea too, this enormous rush of pain and blood as I blacked out and ... quite literally ... died.

"A little too much rum, hey?"

Coming from a long way away, out of limitless galactic blacknesses, spiralling, corkscrewing into the present, opening my eyes to see Uncle Mario standing above me, hand on my shoulder.

It was a bright morning.

I should have been covered with mosquito bites. That was the logical thing, wasn't it? Only looking at my arms, they were totally clean. Doña Teresa just plain old Doña Teresa over at the far end of the dining room, cooking up what smelled like beans.

"He never drinks at home," said Lucia, looking very sexy. An interesting racial mix. A little Indian. A little Italian. Both on top of what began as a mad Hungarian two generations back leaving Budapest, travelling to Sicily, marrying a Sicilian, then finally settling in Peru. "He's not used to it."

"Well, he'll get used to it soon enough. You'd better go into the house and do your things, and then we can have some nice breakfast," said Mario, helping me to my feet. "Are you OK?"

"Fine," I answered and started to walk into the house, Uncle Mario grabbing the carved wooden box he had given me and thrusting it into my hand.

"Don't forget this! A gift is a gift."

Fine, but everything 'different.' Everything in the old house 'different.' The massive living room like a cave, little pieces of antique Indian weaving framed, hanging on the walls, alive for me now, every dot and curve 'speaking' to me, the air itself filled with 'presences.' I thought of Alice in Wonderland, "the slithy toves did gyre and gimble in the wabe ..." Wasn't that the way it went? The dead, hitherto empty air itself seeming to "gyre" and "gimble" around me. I wondered what Lewis Carroll had been 'on' when he wrote Alice. Something, no doubt.

In the washroom I stood looking out of the open window into the surrounding jungle feeling that 'presences' were talking to me, like slithering up and down on a violin E string: "You don't belong to 'them' any more. Now you are one of us." The air itself filled with all sorts of shapes, tenuously visible but on the edge of invisibility.

Let me see if I can reproduce some of them:

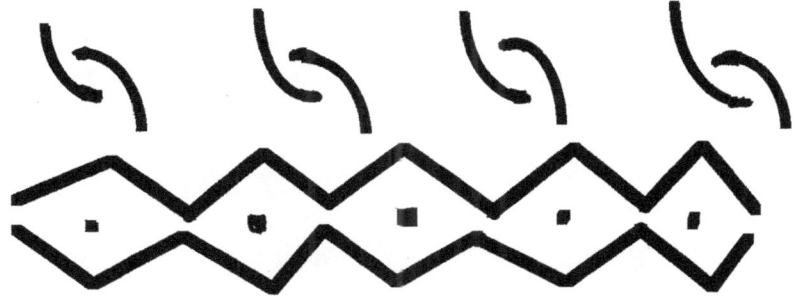

They were all signs that I was very familiar with from Indian pots and weaving, but for the first time they weren't just designs, but part of me, like an extension of my own internal being.

The top design I saw a little differently from what I was used to.

It is an ancient Middle Eastern/Anatolian 'letter-glyph' depicting two copulating snakes. It is written all over the ruins at Tiawanaku as

preceded by ⊙ 〰️ . The ◯ is another ancient Old World letter-glyph for "sun" and has the phonetic value of TI. The two wavy lines (carved into the ruins at Tiawanaku in a variety of forms), 〰️ , is a water letter-glyph with the value of A. So taken together the three 'letter-glyphs' carved into the ruins at Tiawanaku actually spell the name of the place itself – TI-A-NAKU.

Of course when I first saw these equivalences between Old World letters and their equivalents at Tiawanaku, I was uncertain that I was right. How *could* there be any connection between Tiawanaku and ancient Turkey, the Levant, Iraq?

I remember one time when I was having dinner with my Kabbalistic mystic friend, Menke Katz, in Spring Glen, New York. I thought I'd play a little game. I believed that Menke had certain "powers" about him – call it "intuitions." He saw things that no one else saw. I understood ל as NAKU so I wrote it on a napkin and put it in front of The Master.

"Does this mean anything to you?"

It was as if the wisdom of the entire ancient Middle East was sitting there in front of me. Menke didn't hesitate a moment, turned the figure on its side, wrote something else down (and I didn't understand Hebrew at the time and didn't keep the napkin) and proclaimed triumphantly "NAKASH. Hebrew for serpent!"

Oddly enough, the figure that I was seeing pulsating back and forth half in and half out of reality wasn't like the letter-glyph from Tiawanaku, but like the Hopi *Nawach*:

Which, of course, was merely another variation of the same thing – NAKU, NAKASH, NAWACH.

And it shouldn't have been in the Hopi symbol repertory at all, should it? The Hopi are centred in the American Southwest. What possible connection could they have with the mysterious, massive, megalithic pyramids and temples of Tiawanaku in Bolivia? Well, the more you read Hopi myth, the more you understand that there is a connection! First of all, the Hopi say that they originate on the other side of the ocean. They came across the ocean to a great shore (which I take as South America). Then they entered into a cave-world, an Underground, where they lived for a long time. Then they emerged from this cave world. I remember reading other Pueblo Indian myths about this emergence that very specifically say that after their emergence they came to the City of the Gods on the edge of a great lake and that the gods themselves looked exactly the way their Katchinas (divine icons … like Catholic statues of the saints) look. In fact the Katchinas are an attempt to recapture the way the gods looked when they first encountered them. And Hopi myth very specifically says they came from the "red sandstone house in the South." Where could this be? The earliest buildings at Tiawanaku are made of red sandstone. So

... what all these so-called "legends" must mean is that the Hopi came to South America from Southeast Asia across the Pacific, landed on the South American shore, somehow got into some caves under the Andes where they lived for a long time, then they emerged, stayed at Tiawanaku for a while and began their migrations out into the Americas, eventually ending up in the American Southwest... New Mexico.

The symbol for NAKU itself is a representation of two snakes copulating and is an obvious symbol for rebirth. The snake always is.

The fascinating thing about all this is how it relates back to *Gilgamesh*.

In *Gilgamesh* Tiawanaku is called Anaku. The NAKU part of the name is written ⌐┐ on the ruins themselves. And in the poem itself there is a very specific reference to a snake stealing the thorn-apples of immortality and then shedding its skin.

Let me get very specific and scholarly here for a moment and quote *Gilgamesh*.

First there is the name of the thorn-apples:

... Its name shall be 'Man Becomes Young in Old Age.'
I myself shall eat it
And thus return to the state of my youth. *

Secondly there is the episode in the poem of the snake stealing the thorn-apples from Gilgamesh:

Gilgamesh saw a well whose water was cool.
He went down into it to bathe in the water.
A serpent snuffed the fragrance of the plant;
It came up [from the water] and carried off the plant.
Going back it shed [its] slough. **

The snake eats the thorn-apples and sheds its skin ("slough") – one of the most universal symbols in world myth of rebirth/rejuvenation. And here the serpent symbol in Bolivia is used to spell out the very name of the place. What is the NAKU in TIAWANAKU really saying? That *this is the place of rejuvenation and renewal!*

---

* Quoted from *The Ancient Near East: An Anthology of Texts and Pictures* edited by James B. Pritchard. Princeton: Princeton University Press, 1958, p.74.
** The same.

These were some of the thoughts that were going through my mind when I came back into the house and took a shower and changed clothes.

And the other symbol?

Perhaps the most persistent symbol woven into Andean fabrics, the TI in TIAWANAKU, the sun-symbol repeated over and over again.

So, what I was seeing, on the very edge of seeing, was the name of the place traced elusively and half visible in the very air that surrounded me. TI-NAKU, TI-NAKU, TI-NAKU, SUN-SNAKE, SUN-SNAKE. I realized that I was a very different person from the person who had accepted the offer of "herbal tea" from Doña Teresa the night before.

What was all that business of becoming a jaguar all about? My "death" and "resurrection"? Of course I knew. Any ethnologist worth his salt knew about these things. It is the entire basis of ancient religion.

There are two worlds that surround us, the world of the uninitiated and the world of the initiated. To the uninitiated, the world is flat, dull, all surface. But to the initiated suddenly all reality becomes energized and filled with "presences." Sometimes occidental mystics and poets have moments of perception when they see the "real" world under the surface of the ordinary. I think of poems like Coleridge's "The Lime Tree Bower, My Prison," or of Thoreau at Walden saying "I cease to exist and begin to be." Mystic saint-poets like San Juan de la Cruz are very aware of the Other World in the midst of the world of the everyday. Even in a book like The Apocalypse, Book of Revelations, the vision of the City of God is a commonplace to the ancient shaman.

I'd seen the representations of what had happened to me the night before in a thousand places, all over Mochica pots, at Tiawanaku, San Agustín in Colombia, even carved into the cover of the box that Uncle Mario had insisted on giving to me. It is all over ancient Chinese bronzes and carved into Proto-Chavín bone carvings.

So what had been "theory" for me up to now, suddenly became reality, and I slowly began to realize that what Doña Teresa had put me through the night before was some sort of shamanic initiation and that spiritually, inside the essential me, I had become what the Mayas called a Nagual ...

Proto-Chavín Carving of Jaguar Spirit-Helper Killing the "Old Self" of the Individual Being Shamanistically Initiated.

Ancient Chinese Bronze Depicting Same Thing

Mochica Pots Showing Jaguar-Spirit Destroying "The Old Self."

a Were-Jaguar. What Doña Teresa had done was to make me like herself and, I wondered, was Uncle Mario also one of "us"?

My senses were super-heightened.

I'd always had a problem of hypersensitive hearing, always had problems sleeping because, more than anyone else I knew, I could pick up and amplify the slightest street sounds. It was always as if traffic, the sounds of planes, a stereo half a block away, were right in the same room with me. I always wore sun-glasses, even on cloudy winter days because my eyes were very sensitive to light. Even taste, touch ... for me an orgasm was a volcanic eruption of pleasure. And I slept very little. When I lived in Los Angeles, out by the International Airport, I'd wake up in the middle of the night and go down to downtown L.A., or out to the Sunset Strip and sit in a burlesque movie all night long, walk the streets, seek out the company of others like myself, The Sleepless, Super-Tuned-In-Ones. It wasn't a gift but a curse, and I'd always longed to just be 'normal' ... 'ordinary' ... and now it was even worse ... now there were 'presences' out there in the jungle that called to me. I wasn't even hungry. I should say *physically* hungry. What possessed me now were "spirit-hungers," and I felt I *had* to respond to them, that it would be dangerous for me if I didn't respond.

I washed up, did my things, changed clothes and came back into the dining room where everyone was eating, a big mug of coffee and a big plate of beans, meat and rice at my place next to Lucia.

"I've got to talk to you," I said to Lucia in English so that no one else would understand, experiencing a kind of paranoia and distrust that I thought must simply be my new added layers of ... what would you call it, my Nagual instinct? Lucia seemed to be in her element here. I'd complained about the huge suitcase she'd brought with her from Lima, but I couldn't complain now, looking at her in her thonged sandals, black pleated skirt and gauzey black blouse, wearing a matching set of silver earrings and necklace that I'd bought her in Lima. Beautiful filigree. Instant heirlooms for the daughters we would have who still hadn't been conceived.

"What does he want?" asked Mario. Only even Mario wasn't the same for me. I looked at him and saw him more "animal" than "man." The physical face hadn't changed, but I had acquired a new kind/degree of perception and I could see a kind of jaguar "second-self" that he wore like a permanent translucent mask. Just plain old Uncle Mario didn't understand what I'd said, but Nagual Mario did, and while plain old Uncle Mario was asking about what I wanted, the *other* Mario, without a word, but through some sort of meditative projection, very well understood what I wanted and told me "Wait, eat first, satisfy your hungers in the proper order."

"I don't know," said Lucia. What might I want of her and her long black hair and white thighs on this very bright, perfect day in the middle of the Garden of Eden ... ?

"We can eat first," I said, sitting down tasting the meat. Pork, of course, fried in some sort of delicious, salty brown sauce. Whatever else she was, Doña Teresa was an excellent cook.

"What's going on?" she asked. "You seem so 'crazy' today ..."

"I've never felt more sane," I answered as I devoured everything on my plate.

Usually I was very fastidious about my coffee. Lots of cream and sugar, getting it "just right." But now I drank it black, nothing added. It wasn't just that I was thirsty but I wanted my flavours raw and primary.

I finished everything in a few moments and told Lucia "*Te voy a esperar en nuestro cuarto ...*"

"You're embarrassing me," she said. "Sit down."

"*Esta bien,*" said Uncle Mario, as if he had understood what she was saying, although he'd earlier made a point of the fact that he didn't understand a word of English. "It's OK ... *Ustedes los jovenes pueden hacer lo que tienen ganas de hacer* – you young people can do what you want. *Verguenza no existe en esta casa.* Shame doesn't exist in this home."

Lucia laughing. "Do you remember, when I was in school, we were forced to take showers with our clothes on?"

"Don't get me going on dualism! The spirit is good, the flesh evil. It's nothing but a curse. Go ahead."

"First I'm going to take my time eating," she said, strong-willed as always. One thing no one was going to rush her about was eating.

"OK, I'll be in our room," I said, getting up, looking at Doña Teresa at the far end of the hall, looking my way, smiling, very 'jaguarish' herself, very young looking, perfect legs, body, face, as if there were another truer Self enveloping her old lady core, a real versus an illusory her. She didn't say anything but I could still *hear her thoughts.*

"It's wonderful to have you inside the magic circle. Go ahead. She'll be in in a few minutes. I'll see to it!"

The whole air filled with growling. Maybe that's not the word. Call it 'purring,' a deep, self-satisfied, reverberating 'purr,' emanating not only from her but from Uncle Mario as well, and the "others," beyond, circling around us on the other side of Reality.

I went back into the room and stretched out on the bed.

The whole room was white, the stone walls, the bed itself. And the mosquito netting that hung from the ceiling reminded me of a bridal veil. Our sex life up to then had been pretty tame. She really was torn by a dualistic sense that The Flesh was evil and The Spirit was Good. And I wasn't much better, soaked as I had been, in Irish Catholicism all through grammar school, high school and college.

I took off all my clothes and stretched out on the bed smiling to myself, remembering a retreat we'd had at Leo High in Chicago. The retreat master was a Father Dysmus Clark, supposedly named after the Good Thief who was on the cross next to Jesus when he was crucified. At least that's what he told us: "Dysmus was the first man to enter Heaven because of Jesus." And he'd also said, "If you're out on a date with a girl, when you bring her home, don't touch her, don't kiss her, don't get anything started. If you have to kiss something, kiss the cat."

What would the good priest have said now if he'd seen me stretched out naked on a bed waiting for my bride? Kiss the cat, indeed! In a sense now I'd *become* the cat.

Getting impatient. There were so many other things to do. The Spirit World out there was whispering for me to come out into the jungle, "Now that you are one of us."

Things "they" wanted to show me. Signs and miracles (is that what they were saying?) from the times of the gods ...

And then Lucia came in.

"Why are you acting so crazy?" she started in, all set for some sort of fight, big discussion, resistance, debate. That was what radical dualists did, stayed totally inside their heads. That was virtue and sanity – the eternal art of debate.

Only the voices wouldn't let me alone.

"You know what to do," they groaned from the jungle in through the open window, green, sun lit, feline voices, the Other World that forever remains inaccessible until it is unlocked by the taking of the Sacred Drug.

So I slowly got up and took her in my arms, started undressing her.

She never had looked more beautiful. Voluptuous, fleshy, her skin white but with a special orientalesque undertone to it.

"Not during the day, in the light..." she started to say but I stopped her talking with a kiss and gently guided her over to the bed where we made love as we had never made it before, somehow the place, the 'presences,' the moment, allowing her to throw aside all her restraints and give herself up not so much just to me but to the Spirit of the Place. She became the Magna Mater and I was the Young Sun and together we somehow embodied the coming together of Sky and Earth, The Morning-Star-become-Young-Sun splicing with the Spirit of the Earth, every inch of our bodies, every moment, every nuance of pleasure, actualized and augmented as we precipitously hurtled toward sacred satiation. It all happened within a matter of moments, the first time, really, that we had ever come to this sort of fulfilment and satiation, when we were finished still kissing, holding on to each other, then lying back and falling into the sleep of the blessed.

Nine months later our firstborn, our son, Hugh, would be born at the University of Illinois student hospital in Urbana-Champaign.

We slept for a while, but some time around noon I opened my eyes with a strong instinctive urge to go outside. The voices were insistent. There were more things to be revealed. I kissed her lightly. She woke up but didn't want to get up, feeling she had to 'excuse' her sleeping during the day. "I hardly slept at all last night..."

So I left her in bed, got dressed and went back into the dining room, found Doña Teresa in the dining room as if she were waiting for me.

"And Uncle Mario?" I asked.

"*Trabajando*," she answered, smiling, as if guarding deep secrets, always the One Who Knew, the one who seemed to be the servant, but who really ruled the entire *hacienda*, pausing, and then taking me by the hand. "*Vamanos* – Let's go ..."

It was funny, the associations I had brought with me from my past, thought of her for a moment as a witch. Only was she the Evil Witch of the West (sunset) or the Good Witch of the East (Sunrise)? The East! The witch of joy and rebirth!

And, as a matter of fact, the house itself was oriented to the Four Quarters and on the West were the fields where they grew the yucca and manioc, where the orange and grapefruit, mango and papaya groves were, on the East side of the house was the totally untouched jungle. It was almost as if the whole plantation had been planned to coincide with the ancient pre-Columbian symbolism of the year-structure.

Doña Teresa pulled me into the jungle for a way and then stopped and let my hand go.

"*Y ahora tu vas a ser el Conductor* – And now you will be the Conductor."

Frightened for a moment, thinking of the Bardo Conductor in the *Tibetan Book of the Dead*, the 'conductor' who takes dead-souls into the world beyond at the moment of death. Only there wasn't any link between what she had just said and Tibetan necrosymbolism, was there? And I felt that if I could just 'centre' myself, open up the pathways to the centre of my soul, listen to what the Presences had to say, I could pass whatever sort of test Doña Teresa was submitting me to and step one step further in toward the centre of the circle of, what should I call it, INITIATION, ESOTERICA, KNOWLEDGE …

I 'focused' myself as best as I could. Techniques that I borrowed from my years of Zen. Suzuki's *Zen Mind, Beginner's Mind*, my constant companion over the years of painfully inching toward *Satori*.

I closed off the outside world, the birds, the plants, everything around me, until the Voices were speaking inside me instead of from Out There, and I was filled with an overwhelming sense of being 'directed'. Started off to my left, eastward into the densest jungle I had ever seen, under a high canopy of trees, surprisingly comfortable though (the altitude?) … expecting anything …

At first I thought there was barely a path here at all, that we were going into either totally new territory or places that were seldom visited. And then I brushed aside some grass and saw paving stones underneath, perfectly cut, hexagonal, like the bottom stones of so many of the old Inca buildings in Cuzco.

"Inca?" I asked her and she laughed, reached into her pocket and pulled out a dried slice of something. Like dried pineapple but smaller, ugly and withered and black, like a slice (this was my first thought) of testicles.

I was about to toss it into the underbrush only when I lifted my hand she suddenly roared, her roar echoing through the jungle, "Eat it! Eat it now!"

I still hesitated and she lunged toward me and raised up her hand/paw so I put it in my mouth and began to chew.

It was acrid and foul, like chewing on a vinegar-soaked pincushion. I was afraid to swallow, afraid that the 'pins' would puncture my oesophagus and stomach. But she hovered over me now, enormous and threatening, roaring "Swallow it, swallow it, swallow it now …"

So I did, and she relaxed, got ahead of me on the path, automatically expecting me to follow. Which I did. She was on all fours now, mostly jaguar, very little of the human left, shedding her clothes as she went, until she was totally naked, totally feline. There was nothing of the old lady left in her now. And what most impressed me, even more than the transformation of species, was the transformation in *time*. She wasn't just young and vigorous, but ageless, as if she had somehow escaped entirely from the strictures and restrictions of Time. Still part of me wondering if it all was really happening or was it 'dream,' 'hallucination'? We passed a large pool off to our left, steam rising up from the water. All made out of perfectly cut stone, the kind of stonework that I associated with the Incas.

"Inca?" I asked again, and again the same laughter, only this time totally the laughter of a jaguar instead of an old lady. "The Incas were not even dreamt of when this world was built." More roar than speech. Difficult to understand.

We were in the midst of even more dense jungle now, a kind of eternal twilight world, a canopy of high trees blocking out the light. Strangely still, almost cold. I kept thinking of the taboos of the jungle Indians, of places where no one dare go, haunted by evil spirits.

I would have done anything to have simply turned around and gone back, but I knew I'd never get away with it. And I was afraid of her now. Not just her jaguar body but… what must have been her jaguar mind.

We began to ascend a series of stone stairs set in the middle of a steep hill. The stairs reminded me a little of Maya/Khymer temples, Angor Wat or Chichen Itza, Uxmal. But I said nothing as I followed her up to a beautifully paved stone circle on top of the hill, four statues at the four cardinal points, on the South the statue of what at first I took to be the devil, a bull's head and hooves for feet, carrying a trident, the face contorted in anger. The other statues I hardly noticed as she sat me down on a small bench in the middle of the circle, facing the statue of the devil… or maybe not the devil, but the Hindu god Yama, the Maya

Ah Yamas, the Lord of the Underworld, the ancient prototype for all the images of the devil in 'western' myth and theology.

"We stay here until tomorrow morning now," said my jaguar friend handing me another and then another withered slice of what was obviously some sort of psychedelic cactus. I wished that I knew more about the exact nature of the psychedelia of the ancients so I would have known exactly what I was taking. Not that I had much choice. I chewed and swallowed, chewed and swallowed; I remember protesting, saying that Lucia would be worried about me, we had to get back to the *hacienda*, this was madness, but she both threatened and calmed me, "Don't worry, these things happen, it is *that* time of year, of death and resurrection ... you will see ..."

I felt paralysed. I doubt that I could have made my way back to the *hacienda* even if she had let me. The jungle began to 'breathe' for me. It's hard to describe. Nothing was just what it was any more. Everything had 'presences,' everything was spotted, filled with luminous lights and alive. I kept thinking of St. Paul's remarks about seeing God in this life through a glass darkly, and in the next life seeing him face to face. I kept feeling that for me the dark glass had been removed and I was seeing things the way they really were for the first time. It was like being in a room filled with all sorts of 'signals' – radio waves, AM, FM, TV. They were there, but you couldn't perceive them. But they *were* there! If you had the proper receivers you could pick them up. And it was as if now the sacred drugs that I had been eating had enabled me to be able to tune in to All Reality.

At dusk it was as if the whole circle I was sitting in was slowly flooded with water and canoes began to slide in, giant anaconda-shaped canoes that surrounded me, filled with small dark people carrying spears, with little containers around their necks that they'd open from time to time and take a slice of something out of, like the slices of what I guessed was the dried cactus that I myself had taken. They would silently chew on these slices and stand around me, facing the statue of the devil-Yama, Ah Yamas, Yam Cimil, the Lord of the Underworld.

Some time earlier I had speculated that Yama/Ah Yamas, bull-god that he was, was really a symbol of the sun in winter, the sun-bull dwelling in the Underworld.

I was strangely alert, not tired as night came on and the moon emerged in the sky, full enough to illuminate all the strange silent jaguar-men who surrounded me. I had never seen a brighter moon and I don't think it was merely the brightness of the moon that enabled me to see night like day, but something in the 'illuminating' nature of the drug itself that I had taken – and was forced to continue to take.

Time totally disappeared for me and I found myself in what can best be described as a 'continuous, instantaneous Present.' There was no progression, no sense of 'movement' or 'progression.' Reality hung suspended in the Now like bits of fruit in jelly, fish frozen in ice.

And then some time in the midst of this timeless Now, a figure unlike the others appeared in his own anaconda-shaped canoe, a circular headdress of feathers on his head, surrounded by animals, all submissive, totally tame, trained … jaguars and pumas, monkeys, birds perched on his shoulders.

Everything stayed 'frozen,' no before or after, just more intensified present.

The 'animal master' (which is how I saw him – The Master of the Animals) approached me at one point in this timeless continuum and took a little container off his belt, dipped his thumb in it and drew four figures on my face, forehead, chin and both cheeks.

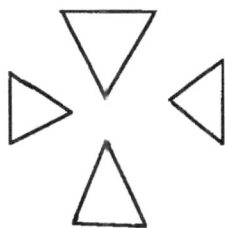

I wanted to ask him or Doña Teresa what it meant, what was going on, but found myself unable to speak or even move.

I sat there totally immobile through what could have been centuries or merely a moment, I couldn't say which, and then, when the sky began to lighten in the east, everyone became agitated, the whole forest came alive and a stairway appeared in the middle of the stone circle. That's the only way I can describe it – a stairway appeared in the middle of the stone circle where I had been sitting. Doña Teresa had taken me over to the side of the circle and stood with me as I saw the stairway materialise, and as the first rays of the sun began to emerge from the east like swords or spears of fire, sunlight as I had never seen it before, all my ghostly companions dipped into the circular containers (made out of bark? leather?) around their necks and pulled out wafers, put them in their mouths and started to chew, and the man I had begun to think of as the Master of Animals nodded to Doña Teresa/Doña Jaguar and she gently nudged me forward toward the stairs.

I wasn't really sure if they were there or merely in my head. And I'm still not sure. In fact to this day I'm not sure whether anyone else was there in the stone circle, any *one* or any *thing*. For all I know it was *all* an hallucination and I had never left the *hacienda* at all.

But it hardly seemed to matter whether I was ascending a real or an imaginary stairway as I ascended to the top and could see a brilliant white, snow-capped mountain to my right and a lake to my left and I somehow understood as if silent words had been spoken to me inside my mind/understanding – THIS IS THE WORLD-MOUNTAIN AND THE WORLD-SEA, WE ARE AT THE CENTRE OF THE WORLD NOW … AND NOW YOU MUST DIE …

Oddly enough when I heard/understood that I was about to die, I was totally unafraid. It wasn't merely indifference either, but almost a positive anticipation of some great, further transformation that was about to occur. Death wasn't Death any more, nor Life, Life. Everything was transformative and plastic. I had gone through one ritual death and resurrection already and changed substantially – was that merely the beginning of a death-resurrection ('growth,' 'spiritual enlargement') series?

Teresa had grown in stature and towered over me now, stood behind me and orientated me toward the rising sun, and when the first rays of the sun fell on my face she reached over my shoulders and began to claw at my chest, ripping off the skin, then clawing into the ribs, twisting me around and throwing me down on my back, her mouth at my throat in what first seemed like a kiss, but turned out to be a fatal clamping down of her jaws on my trachea, ripping my whole throat open, then dismembering me, arms ripped from my shoulders, disembowelling me, 'killing' me, but at the same time it was as if there was another me standing watching the whole murder, not being murdered but merely as a spectator. Then there was a moment of total blank. I was dead … it was something I had never experienced before, much more complete than that first 'shadow-death.' Not unconsciousness, not dream, but a total absence of any sense of Self. I simply *wasn't*. It was less than blank. It was non-ness.

Which lasted for what could have been forever for all that I knew There wasn't even an 'I' *to* know. Then slowly I began to come back into the Now. Through a kind of delta-shaped door in the horizon, back to the Here and Now:

△

Only not as 'me,' the old human me; this time I too was a jaguar, covered with short fur, thick neck and clawed paws, smelling and seeing, 'feeling' more intensely than I had ever felt before. And all the 'shadow' figures that had come in the canoes were jaguars too now. It was a whole congregation of jaguars, the Master of Animals now no longer a Master of Animals but the largest, most dominant jaguar of all.

"Anak, Nak, the place in the middle," Doña Teresa growled into my ear as we descended from the top of the pyramid, and when I looked back I saw it slowly dissolve as the other jaguars got back into their canoes and half-human, half-jaguar, paddled off into the forest, the giant Master of Animals jaguar putting his immense half-paw, half-hand on my shoulder and growl-talking to me, "Now you will be forever one of us. You will never be the same again."

Slowly, as we made our way back to Uncle Mario's place, loping along through the jungle, I could feel my body changing back to its human form. Or (what I really believe), it hadn't changed form at all, but the whole metamorphosis was purely illusory, pure hallucination. It *seemed* to me, though, that when we started making our way back to the *hacienda* I was running along on all fours and that slowly I started changing back first to some sort of ape-like form, with my long arms on the ground, slowly becoming totally biped again, so that when we walked into the kitchen/dining room, what Lucia and Uncle Mario saw was just me and an old Indian woman coming in from a walk in the jungle.

"What happened with you two? Lucia just told me that you weren't here at home last night…"

"We got lost," lied Doña Teresa, and we sat down and ate breakfast as if nothing at all had changed.

Doña Teresa went back to the stove and started cooking again, and we all sat down and ate. There was strong coffee, cocoa, cornbread, guava jelly, sausages. Everything normal. On the surface. But inside I *was* changed forever. I felt 'jaguarish.' My perceptions were permanently heightened. I heard birds I had never heard before, tasted tastes that I had never before tasted, smelled smells that I had never smelled before. Or perhaps I had heard, tasted, smelled the same things before, but now quality (intensity) had actually changed the identities of things.

But as far as Lucia was concerned, nothing had changed, I was just the same old me doing and saying the same old things. And I almost accepted Mario's offer, a few days later, the day before we were supposed to leave.

"Why don't you stay here with us, Hugo. It's a simple life. But there's more than enough of everything. You can help me with the *hacienda*.

Maybe I can even learn a little English to talk to the birds with!"

He laughed his hearty laugh, glancing from time to time at Doña Teresa over in the corner washing dishes, the very soul of humility and industriousness, as if he really knew what had happened, on a whole other level was in on the secret, and the offer to stay there with him was really an offer to stay permanently in the midst of the jaguar-shaman world.

But there was another 'me' inside that had other agendas.

I had been changed, yes, but there were still whole territories in me that may have been touched, but not eliminated. So I refused Mario's offer.

"Class will be starting soon now, I just can't 'disappear,' I have my commitments, you know ..."

"We all disappear," he said, looking even more forcibly at Doña Teresa, who refused to look back, "at least most of us ..."

I followed his gaze over to Doña Teresa, wondering how old she really was, seventy, seven hundred, seven thousand. When had the jaguar-people first discovered the life-prolonging qualities of their cacti and mushrooms, their various "fleshes of the gods," which was a literal translation of the Aztec Teonanacatl? And if these cacti and mushrooms *didn't* prolong life, why call them the flesh of the gods? Only the gods could claim immortality!

So we returned to Los Angeles where I was teaching American literature at Loyola-Marymount – which was then simply called Loyola.

To all intents and purposes everything was normal.

Lucia had her first baby, a boy who my parents (living in Sun City, now far from Los Angeles, my father a retired M.D.) insisted on calling with my father's and my name – so he became Hugh B. Fox III. Which I always think is almost funny, because I am Junior ... and it almost makes my son sound older than me. Doesn't Hugh B. Fox III sound like he carries more weight than Hugh B. Fox Jr.?

We had two more children in two more years, Cecilia and Marcella.

I had begun a book on Henry James and was teaching one course a term of American literature plus a couple of courses of Freshman Comp. We bought a little house on Jenny, right next to the L.A. International Airport in Westchester, bicycling distance from the university – and I began what was to become the strangest time in my life.

Lucia had a job teaching Spanish at San Fernando State University – which meant a long forty-five minute drive each way to and from work. I was 5 minutes away from Loyola. We had separate bedrooms. Neither of us could sleep in the same bed (even the same room) with anybody else.

She'd go to bed every night at eleven or twelve and I'd try to do the same, take a bath, relax, read a little, go into my room and try to sleep. But I never could. It was as if the jaguar voices were still calling me, whispers and growls in the Amazonian forests of my mind. I remember, I went out and bought black suede boots and black corduroy trousers and a black knit shirt, a black suede jacket, leather cap. What were the voices saying? I could never make out words, but it was as if I were being directed from the inside. I would try to sleep for a couple of hours, then get up, get in the car and start to "explore the night." That's the best way I can put it.

Sometimes I would drive to downtown Los Angeles, park the car off in the warehouse district and walk over to Main Street. Which in those days was alive all night long. Burlesque movie houses, porn stores. Ironically just a couple of blocks from the Catholic Cathedral.

Sometimes I'd go into a porn movie, filled mainly with bums who were trying to sleep as Betty Page was up there on the big screen taking it all off as coquettishly as possible – the Coy Seductress.

I'd stay for a while, but quickly get bored, go out into the streets again, back in the car, drive down to Malibu or Venice, walk along the beach, no idea what I was 'supposed' to be doing, no idea of where I was 'supposed' to go, just a powerful, vague, inarticulate drive inside me that wouldn't let me sleep.

I didn't talk to anyone or bother anyone, no one talked to or bothered me.

Of course I looked pretty tough I guess, a black panther stalking around through the streets, wandering along the beach. What was it all about? Was it just the physiological effects of the drugs, or was some sort of 'message' being formed inside me? Had I been chosen by 'the gods' to discover some sort of secret there in the middle of the dead, menacing night?

I would stay out almost until dawn, then drive back home and sleep a few hours, be up in time for my eight o'clock class. Sometimes I'd sleep between classes, put a blanket on the floor of my office and stretch out and sleep for an hour or two, somehow get through the day. But I was getting only a few hours of sleep a day.

I remember going to Confession to Father Von der Ahe one time. He was a psychologist as well as a Jesuit and, as a matter of fact, his father was one of the wealthiest men in Southern California, the founder of Von's chain of food stores. The library at Loyola-Marymount is the Von der Ahe library. That's where the money came from.

I went to Confession, but I didn't have anything to really confess. It wasn't a sin to be a night wanderer. Father Von der Ahe became impatient with me:

"What exactly do you have to confess?"

"I don't know ... I took some drugs when I was in South America recently. I went through some sort of 'initiation,' became a jaguar shaman."

"I would suggest you see a psychiatrist, perhaps get on some medication. You seem to be in some sort of manic state. What concerns me isn't so much the manic phase, but the depressive phase that inevitably follows. If I were you I would anticipate what was coming before it arrived. I would think you need medication."

Which may have been good advice, but I never took it, merely continued to wander – wander the streets, Sunset Boulevard, over to MacArthur Park, still down to the beach, Palos Verdes ... and then one night about six months after my insomnia began, I was sitting on the beach at Venice under a full moon, facing the surf, and I felt myself slowly being surrounded by, how can I put it, a 'presence.'

I looked around honestly expecting to be surrounded by a 'gang' of some sort.

Only there was no one there, and at the same time the 'presence' wouldn't go away but hovered around me like black beating wings.

And then the voices began.

"Who are the voyagers, where is the sea, where are they going, to you or to me? Who are the voyagers and why do they voyage, the centre of nowhere, the twin solstice boys?"

It was gibberish as far as I was concerned and I got up and turned away from the surf to confront what had become a huge amorphous kind of black 'cloud' in front of me. I was at the end of my patience. I was possessed, only by what demons? If they had orders for me, they would have to be more specific, I was tired of the hidden nature of the 'presence' that pursued me and disallowed me any rest. My whole career and my marriage were starting to suffer. How was I supposed to finish my James book without sleep or even time for research? And research was the core to survival in the academic wars!

I advanced toward the cloud in front of me and suddenly it shifted, moved, assumed the shape of a giant black jaguar and threw me down on my back on the sand and white fangs materialized out of the blackness as phantom jaws clamped down on my neck again and I felt myself 'dying' once more, passing into the Zero Zone, no forward or backward, no sense of being, existing at all ... and then as I slowly came back to myself I opened my eyes. It was seven-thirty and the sun was out. There was no time for me to go home and change. I would have to go to class dressed all in black, boots and jacket and all – and there was a definite word in my mind, as if it had been imprinted, stamped with a rubber stamp. The word was ANAKU, and next to it, another word was stamped, much less clearly, but still legible – GILGAMESH.

I went to class. I remember my boss, Ted Erlandson, laughing at my outfit:
"I hope you're not turning into a hippy! Or have you joined a motorcycle gang?"

You can imagine the stares I received. It was a pretty conservative place in those days, all Jesuits and lay professors. The nuns still hadn't arrived – except as students. Although my students for Freshman Comp were pretty "cool cats," if I may say so. Remember at the end of The Graduate, the blond boyfriend? Well, the guy that played that part was one of my students – Brian Avery. He also had a short spot on screen in The Four Horses of the Apocalypse – the role of a German aviator. He never made it big, but a lot of my former students went into control-room jobs, not in front of but behind the cameras. So I had no problem with the students, and afterwards went over to the library and ran into Frank Sullivan, one of the greatest scholars I've ever known (a St. Thomas More scholar who had edited the complete works of More before the Yale edition had ever been even thought of) and I asked him, "Does the word 'Gilgamesh' mean anything to you?"

He motioned me over to the card catalogue. Titles. Found the right drawer and thumbed through it... stepped back ... there it was ... *Gilgamesh*.

"It's a Sumerian poem, actually the first 'epic' as such that has survived."
"What's it about?" I asked.
"It's a voyage story."
"To where?"
"Supposedly across the 'ocean.' In fact that's a large part of the text – the voyage itself."

I was impatient. He had the answers that I needed. My demons began to growl inside me. It was as if I were possessed, and somehow the existence of my possessors depended on my unravelling their riddles.

"But where exactly?"
"Patience! Patience!" smiled Sullivan. I suppose I must have seemed pretty crazy to him, although he hadn't said a word about my clothes, walking over, sitting down at one of the study tables, pulling out a chair

for me, motioning for me to sit down. "It has always struck me, when I was reading *Gilgamesh*, that it completely contradicts our ideas of what we think the ancients believed about the ocean – that it ended and you fell off the edge. Gilgamesh's voyage has always struck me as almost 'reportorial,' and certainly seems to partake of our modern notions of geography, nothing to do with oceans that ended in precipes …"

"But where is the voyage to?" I insisted.

He looked me straight in the eye, obviously curious as to why the answer to this particular scholarly question had such urgency for me.

"The voyage is to Anaku, the tin lands on the other side of the world."

Anaku, the tin lands on the other side of the world.

"Thanks, Frank," I told him, got up and went into the rest room, found a stall and got in, sat down on the toilet and cried silly tears of exactly what, joy … ? Fulfilment?

Of course I knew where Anaku was. I had been there. If you go across the ocean from ancient Iraq, where the Sumerians lived, either around Africa or through the Mediterranean through the Pillars of Hercules and across the Atlantic that way, where are the tin-lands?

There is very little tin in the world. There was tin in ancient England, Sumatra … and Bolivia. And there, in the centre of the Bolivian tin country was one of the strangest, most enigmatic ruins in the world, megalithic pyramids and statues that totally confounded the Spaniards when they arrived there. I remembered Pedro Cieza de León in his book on the Incas asking himself "Who could have built these ruins? Who could have moved these stones? And why was it built here? What function did it serve?"

And the name of this ruin? Tiawanaku.

Anaku.

(Tiaw)anaku.

Of course it was the same place.

So what did it mean, that people from Iraq, the Sumerians, had been to Tiawanaku five thousand years ago?

I was more confused and distraught than ever. I took the poem out of the library and that night went home and read the whole thing and a whole new world of ideas opened up for me.

There are two voyagers journeying across the ocean to Tiawanaku/Anaku, Gilgamesh himself and a friend of his, Enkidu; only Enkidu dies and Gilgamesh goes on a quest for a "thorn-apple" that grows at the bottom of a lake, a "thorn-apple" that is called "makes old men young again".

That's what the text read – a thorn-apple that *makes old men young again*.

So there was some sort of link between Tiawanaku and immortality. It was obviously the same drug (cactus) that Doña Teresa had been feeding me. Only why Tiawanaku?

I thought I would sleep that night after I had finished reading the poem, that the Powers that surrounded me would have mercy on me. I was exhausted and confused and wanted only to slip quietly into sleep and leave this whole business behind for some hours at least.

Only it was not to be, and some time about two or two-thirty I got up and drove down to the beach again, down by the Playa del Rey Marina, and started walking along the sand, the voices again bubbling up, hissing through the sound of the surf, feeling that I would fight back should the Presences materialise into any sort of jaguar shape and attempt again to subdue/destroy me. This suspension of life that I had experienced three times now, for however short a time, was the most horrible experience that I had ever gone through in my life. And who could say whether I would ever wake up again?

I walked down to the water's edge, the moon out almost full again, closed my eyes and listened, sat down on the wet sand, let the waves curl up around me. And the voices began. Were they coming from inside me or from Out There? It was impossible to say. My interior space was outer space. It was as if I were dematerialising and becoming a molecular part of the night itself:

Two there are and will always be,
up to the centre, never three,
seek in the one and you will find two,
Odysseus the Ithacan, Prometheus, you ...

It was worse than nothing. A total blank. Obviously I was being referred back to *The Odyssey*. I had had a course in the Classic Epic when I was working for my M.A. at Loyola in Chicago and had read *The Odyssey* (*Gilgamesh*, I guess, wasn't considered 'classical' enough for Professor Abel) ...

I don't know how long I sat there, but when I got up I was shivering and wet, dawn was just beginning to appear in the eastern sky.

I went home, slept for a while, and then taught my classes and afterwards, instead of going to my office, something new happened, a first – the Spirits began to possess me during the day. Noon became like two a.m. and I slipped into a kind of trance, things totally out of my control, 'presences' surrounding me, out to my car, as if I weren't driving at all, but being driven by 'forces' who knew exactly where they wanted to take me. Out to Westwood, to UCLA, the UCLA library, which I had been using a lot for research on my James book. They'd given me a library card. I was very at home there, in the English and American literature section. That wasn't where I was being directed toward now, though, but toward the area on ancient cultures, the Greeks .... finding myself in the stacks, my handing reaching for a book by a scholar I had never heard of before – Kerenyi. The book – *Prometheus*. Flipping through the pages to an exact spot, a whole section in which Kerenyi says that hidden in the person of Odysseus from Ithaca is another figure, Prometheus as Ithacos, the firegod ... and Prometheus the fire-god in turn is associated with metallurgy ... and has a twin ... Epimetheus. Prometheus is the Morning Star god, Epimetheus the Evening Star god. Prometheus looks forward toward the rising sun, Epimetheus looks backward toward the setting sun. They are twins, two aspects of the same planet – Venus.

Hadn't the first 'message' talked about twins? Twin "solstice boys?"

I went down to the reference section and got a map of South America and located Tiawanaku up in the Andes not far from La Paz in Bolivia, not exactly on but very close to the Tropic of Capricorn.

What was the relationship between the Tropic of Capricorn and the solstices?

The tropics, according to the astronomy books, were those spots on the earth's surface which are specifically referred to as "solstitial points," the extreme points of the sun's journey up and down the surface of the earth during a solar year. So the Tropics, in a sense, were the pivot-points of the sun during a solar year. And *The Odyssey*; what was the whole point of *The Odyssey*? It was about the voyage of Odysseus to ... yes, the Land of the Sun-King.

The Land of the Sun-King where Helios (and later, his son, Æëtes) lived.

I remember sitting down on the floor of the stacks at UCLA in a kind of trance, my head spinning, voyaging across the ocean to the home of Helios, the sun-king, my mind flooding with all sorts of old associations and memories, things that I hadn't thought about for decades.

Of course, in Germanic myth Wotan, the king of the gods, is a sun-god. He is the one-eyed "wanderer." Like the cyclopes. Other sun-god symbols. One eyed gods, the sun's eye (day's eye) wandering through the sky. And Valhalla, Wotan's home ... there was a tree there too, cared for by the goddess Freya. And as long as the gods ate the apples on Freya's tree they were ageless; the moment they stopped eating them, they began to age.

It was the same as in *Gilgamesh*. The thorn-apples that made old men young again in Gilgamesh and in the Germanic legends were the same as Freya's apples of immortality. And as long as the gods ate them they didn't die ... or even age ...

It was a rather obvious equation for me. These drugs were the drugs of immortality.

There was a tree in Valhalla that was the world-tree. A world-snake, the Middle Earth Snake (Mitsgarthwurm) ... it had been decades and decades since I had studied opera in Zerlina Muhlman Metzger's All Children's Grand Opera classes when I was a kid in Chicago and fallen in love with Wagner and had spent hours and hours poring over the scores as I listened to the music on records, reading the English but always referring back to the German, wanting to get inside the Wagnerian mystique as much as possible.

Now suddenly it all made sense – the Land of the Sun-King (Valhalla) was a real place and it was where it was because of its closeness to the Tropic of Capricorn, the pivot-point of the sun during the solar year. Call it the House of the Sun, the Land of the Sun-King. And where the Sun-King himself had lived was Anaku/Tiawanaku ...

Some student came by pushing a cart full of books. Reshelving books, I guess.

There I was on the floor.

"Are you OK?" she asked, looking a little fearful. I hate to think how I looked. I'd hardly been eating and sleeping. The pictures of me taken at the time, in fact, I think show something of my new jaguar nature. I look wild, my eyes staring. The jaguar nature was definitely taking over.

"I'm fine. Just reading ..." I answered, getting up, wanting to leave, go back home, sleep for a while. I still had my late afternoon class in American Literature to teach. Thoreau's *Walden*. Which I knew backwards and forwards; but I still wanted/needed some time to organise my thoughts.

I started to move toward the elevators, my mind crackling with ideas.

The basis for the ancient epics was a voyage across the ocean to either the TinLands or The Land of the Sun-King. The voyage was made by twins who were symbols for Venus as Morning and Evening Star. And the voyage itself was to the Solstice Point – the House of the Sun. When you actually voyaged to the Solstice Point/Tin-Lands, what was there now? Ancient cyclopean ruins.

Then something else suddenly occurred to me. When Gilgamesh goes looking for the thorn-apple that makes old men young again, he finds it but it is eaten by a snake, which then immediately sheds its skin ... an obvious symbol for rebirth.

Odysseus never gets to the Land of the Sun-King. That's the crazy thing about *The Odyssey*; it's about a voyage that never is completed.

But there was another Greek epic about a voyage across the ocean to the Land of the Sun-King – The *Argonautica* – *The Voyage of the Argos*. Jason does complete the voyage and there in the Land of the Sun-King is a tree guarded by a dragon, and the daughter of the Sun-King, Medea, helps Jason drug the dragon so that he falls asleep, so that Jason can steal the golden fleece that are hanging on the tree.

Only trees don't have golden fleece on them.

What they have is apples. And the right 'trees' have the right kind of apples – the thorny apples of immortality.

I was standing in front of the elevator when suddenly all my years of Greek in high school paid off and I remembered some obscure comments by Brother Breen, my Greek teacher, about the similarity of the words for fleece and apples in ancient Greek. Something like our word *melon* – melon-something ... as if the author, Apollonius Siculus, had made a mistake and written "fleece" where he should have written "apples." Or some later scribe had made a mistake in recopying the manuscript.

The earliest epic, *Gilgamesh*, told it the way it should be. It was the correct, canonical form. There was a tree, a serpent, a garden and (here Apollonius was on target) ... a woman.

It was the Garden of Eden image, wasn't it?

The Garden of Eden episode in Genesis was really about Tiawanaku, Bolivia.

Adam wasn't a twin. There was a slight variation – the twins came in in the next generation ... Cain and Abel.

Only in Genesis the whole nature of the 'apples' changed. They were no longer the apples of immortality but the apples of the tree of Good and Evil. In Genesis the serpent tells Eve that if she eats an apple on the tree of Good and Evil she won't die, as God has said, but she shall become *like* God: "And the serpent said unto the Woman: 'Ye shall not surely die. For God doth know that in the day ye eat thereof, then your eyes shall be opened, and ye shall be as God, knowing good and evil" (Genesis, Chapter III).

Which is exactly the opposite of what the apples were everywhere else. In Genesis they become the apples of death instead of the apples of immortality. Whereas the truth was that eating the apples, as I had done, didn't exile me from Eden, but turned the whole world around me, no matter where I was, into a kind of second Eden ... and given me energy that I never would have dreamed of before. In a sense, I thought, as I pushed the Down button for the elevator, Genesis was exactly the opposite of what the apples were really all about. The ancient legends that had filtered out of India and become the basis for Germanic myth reflected much more faithfully than Genesis what the apples of immortality meant for the ancients. They didn't spell out *death* but *eternal life*. But in a way I could understand why Genesis had been changed the way it had. The Jews were the only monotheists of the ancient world. All other ancient cultures saw the world inhabited by multiple gods, divine presences in everything. The way I had begun to see the world. A god of the sea, wind-god, moon god/goddess, sun-god. Everything around me filled full time with a sense of the divine. You couldn't be *allowed* to see The Real as it really was if you were to become a monotheist – so psychedelic cacti and/or mushrooms were prohibited. What I had done, thanks to Doña Teresa, was to have returned to Eden and eaten of the Tree of Good and Evil and in my own mind, based on my own personal experience, had changed its name from Good and Evil to the Tree of Immortality/Enlightenment.

In a way what the serpent had told Eve was true. If you ate the magic thorn-apples, you *did* see the world the way God saw it, in a sense became a minor god yourself.

The elevator came and I made it to the first floor. Only when I tried to walk out back to my car, the Powers took over again and I found myself being pulled and tugged by invisible forces, directed to Special Collections/Rare Books. And when I stood in front of the Special Collections librarian it wasn't my voice but *theirs* that actually spoke.

"I'm looking for a book by Alexander von Humboldt, *Researches Concerning the Institutions and Monuments of the Ancient Inhabitants of America* ..."

Again I could see fear in her face. She wasn't at all sure about me. But somehow she managed to control herself and her professionalism took over. She went over to the card catalogue and "Yes ... as a matter of fact we do happen to have it. It's a rather rare book. London, 1814. Do you have a library card?"

What did she expect me to pull out of my pocket, a clawed hand to rip open her throat? Only the hand that came out of my pocket was very ordinary, with an ordinary library card in it. Which obviously reassured her. Los Angeles was, is and always will be filled with dangerous crazies.

She went and got the book for me and I sat down at one of the reading tables and placed it in front of me, made myself totally passive, silenced my own will, let Them totally take over; and my hand lifted up with a life of its own and opened the old book to page 329 – which contained a comparative table of ancient zodiacs.

I didn't understand and sat there totally confused, the librarian still preoccupied with me, coming over and asking me if everything was all right.

I nodded yes.

"Yes, everything's fine …"

My eyes being directed down to Leo the Lion in the column titled Hindu-Greek Zodiac, moving over to the Mexican Day Sign column where it read "Tecapatl-Silex/Knife-Flint," and then over to the Hindu Lunar Mansion column which read "razor."

HINDU-GREEK ZODIAC	MEXICAN DAY SIGNS	HINDU LUNAR MANSIONS
LION	TECAPATL-SILEX KNIFE-FLINT	RAZOR

I had no idea of what I was supposed to see, but sat there staring, still passive, waiting for my voices to speak. Which they slowly finally did, unwinding, unfurling, hissing like snakes – *The Mansions of the Moon are the Days of the Sun, Razor-Flint Knives that cut no one, the journey through water is a journey through the sky, the stars a map, the reason why…*

I sighed a sigh of … what? Despair, I suppose, despair and frustration.

The librarian, a small woman with her black hair up on top of her head filled with pencils, reminding me of a Japanese Geisha coiffure, came over and asked me:

"Are you finding everything OK?"

"Puzzles," I said. "Conundrums."

"Well, I guess that's what research is all about," she smiled.

I made some notes on the back of an envelope I had in my pocket, a letter, as a matter of fact, from Uncle Mario in Peru. I was even surprised that there was mail service into the jungle where he lived. Probably some trucker, someone with a boat on the river that ran through his property took the letter to Cuzco for him. He had written asking me yet again to come back. And it was very tempting to go back. Obviously his jungle hideaway was, if not *the* source of all these ancient myths, somehow connected with them. There was Eden/Tiawanaku/Anaku, the centre, but the whole continent was obviously connected with it. It had all been part of the same vast cultural complex – when Tiawanaku wasn't a ruin but was actually functioning as the House of the Sun.

It was interesting to see how the Hindu Mansions, the Hindu *lunar* zodiac, had become the Aztec *day*-signs, a strange transformation, indeed, but one that showed the intimate, ancient connections between Meso-America and ancient India.

I made my notes, handed the book back to the librarian and started to leave the library again. But it wasn't to be. There was obviously something else that I was supposed to see that same day, some other connection that had to be made. And I was 'forced' back into the stacks again, the area devoted to mythology, past books on world myth, British folklore, Bolivian folklore and myth, African, Japanese … until I found myself standing in front of a whole series of shelves filled with small red-bound volumes – *The Journal of American Folklore*.

Vol.42, finding my hands flipping the pages to an article on Hopi Tales collected by a researcher named Alexander Stephens.

It was a story about two twins, the sons of the sun, going to visit their father, the Sun. Which, I thought, must be the Morning and Evening Star again. That's what the twins were, wasn't it? The Morning and Evening stars? They get to the House of the Sun which, I thought, must be Tiawanaku again. Only Sun isn't there and Sun's wife hides them. Sun comes back home and he smells the two twins, exactly like the giant in the sky in Jack and the Beanstalk. Was Jack and the Beanstalk a popular version of the same story? Another myth that had emerged from India with the Indo-European peoples who had made their way to England thousands and thousands of years before?

Only in one of the stories of the twins going to the House of the Sun, they meet a Flint-Monster named Cha'veyo, a monster wearing stone/flint arrowheads strung across his chest as a kind of armour.

The associations began to come together for me. The constellation/zodiac symbol of Leo, the Lion, in the Hindu-Mexican system was Flint/Knife. Now I had the twins meeting a Flint Monster. They were meeting Leo, the Lion. The Morning and Evening Stars/Venus meeting Leo/Flint. Or *meeting* wasn't the right word, was it? The right words were "passing through." The sun, accompanied by Venus, passes through the zodiac through the solar year.

Suddenly I remembered another myth about a hero going across the ocean, not to the Land of the Sun-King but to the Islands of the Blessed, the Hesperides, where he found one of the daughters of the Hesperides next to a tree with magic apples on it guarded by a serpent. Another version of Genesis. Only here the hero was Herakles.

Herakles in Greek myth, Hercules in Roman myth.

And if I remembered it correctly, Herakles/Hercules was one of the passengers on the Argos on its way to the Land of the Sun-King, only he gets off and makes his own journey across the ocean.

One of the labours of Herakles/Hercules is to kill the Nemean Lion.

Which must mean that Herakles/Hercules as Sun-God, is passing through the sign of Leo the Lion. In fact the entire story, in all its different versions, must be zodiac stories, and all the episodes in all the myths must be dramatizations of the Sun + Venus, passing through the different zodiac signs.

Only why frame the whole story in this way? What was its relation to Tiawanaku?

And then I remembered a book by Rosemary Grimble about her father's work on myths in relation to ancient voyages in the South Seas: *Migrations, Myths and Magic from the Gilbert Islands*.

The idea was that the ancient sea voyagers in the South Seas would make up stories about the stars to use as navigational guides. They navigated by the stars, the heavens were a giant map for them, which they then turned into stories that could be memorised so that when they were voyaging they could remember the stories and know exactly which way to go.

Could it have been that that's what the zodiac was all about?

Could the zodiac, in fact, have been invented as a star chart to guide ancient mariners across the ocean to the so-called New World? And then had all the epics and myths been derived from these star-charts, so that Jason's and Odysseus' and Herakles' and Gilgamesh's adventures have nothing at all to do with the 'real' world but are all derived from the sun's 'adventures' passing through the sky during a solar year? And did the zodiac point to the House of the Sun, Tiawanaku? Did it mean that Tiawanaku, before it had become an enigmatic lost ruin in the middle of nowhere (the way the Spaniards found it and considered it) had actually been the centre of all ancient myth (and reality)? And then the same myth had been picked up by the ancient Jews and incorporated into Genesis (via the Babylonians, who, in turn, had taken the myths from the Sumerians), and twisted to fit the revolutionary needs of a monotheism that needed to outlaw all psychedelic drugs, truly make man 'mortal,' so that he could not become a god himself, but would have to depend on the new Creator God who had been in direct conflict with his creatures who themselves were striving for (and finding?) their own immortality?

Troy, after all, was in Turkey, just above Mesopotamia. If the Mesopotamians in 3,000 B.C. based their epics on stories of voyaging to Anaku/Tiawanaku, why shouldn't the Trojans at the same time have also voyaged to the New World?

Atacama Desert

Troy III – 3,000 B.C.

If I was right, the whole of ancient history would have to be changed and Tiawanaku would have to be changed from *Nowhere* to *The Very Centre of Ancient Mediterranean/Middle Eastern Myths*.

I got back to Loyola at four-thirty and, of course, my students had all already left and my boss, Ted Erlandson, was sitting in the empty room waiting for me.

"How you doing, Hugh? Come on in, sit down ..."

I went in and sat down.

"I was over at UCLA doing research. I got held up," I said lamely.

"On what?" he asked.

I took the envelope out of my pocket that I'd been writing notes on. Hardly notes at all, more like confused, unintelligible scrawls. He wasn't very impressed.

"I've just discovered that Tiawanaku, Bolivia was the Home of the Sun King in all ancient myths," I said.

"Tia-what?"

"Tiawanaku. The Sumerians called it Anaku."

He stood up, a great big tall guy, lots of beard. He looked like an old Viking wearing the wrong kinds of clothes.

"The Sumerians called someplace in Bolivia Anaku, huh?"

"That's right. And that's where Odysseus was going in *The Odyssey*, it's the Land of the Sun-King in *The Argonautica*, where Herakles was going, the Islands of the Hesperides ... the Garden of Eden in Genesis. Only the apples on the Tree of Good and Evil didn't bring death, the way the bible says, but they were the apples of immortality, like in Germanic myth, the apples that Freya takes care of and when the tree gets chopped down the gods begin to age ..."

"Listen, Hugh," he said, coming over and putting his hand on my shoulder, "I'm beginning to 'hear' things about you. It's OK when you begin to 'hear' things about people, but the kinds of things I'm hearing aren't good. I got a call from Father Von der Ahe today ..."

"He broke the seal of Confession," I protested.

"You didn't really have anything to confess, from what I gather," he answered, sitting down again. "He just cares about you, that's all, thinks you might need a little help. And then that weird outfit you've been wearing around to class ..."

"One day!" I said.

"Whatever," he answered. He wasn't a bad guy. Very fatherly. "Is there anything I can do? Maybe a little counselling wouldn't hurt, a visit to a psychiatrist, some medication. We don't want you to do anything crazy. For your good and the good of the university ..."

"No, I'm OK," I insisted.

"Ever since you got back from Peru," he continued. "Did something especially bizarre happen to you down there?"

"I got interested in the ancient Americas," I lied.

"Of course, you're not here to teach anything about the ancient Americas," he countered, "you're here to teach American literature. And that's not very ancient, I'm afraid."

"OK," I answered, trying to be brisk and offhanded about the whole thing. "Enough said."

Only I guess I wasn't very convincing. He got up again, as sympathetic and paternal as he could be.

"I just want you to be OK," he repeated, "you ... and us ... the whole community. You can understand that."

"No problem," I answered and that was that.

He left, I went to my office and called home. The kids were in school all day until three and then went to a special nursery school where I usually picked them up at five thirty. Lucia was home. She had had the afternoon off and was working on a book on Sor Juana de la Cruz. I had to always give her credit. She was (and still is) one of the greatest scholars I have ever met.

I had called to tell her I'd be right home, but as soon as I dialled our home number it was as if my office was filled with immense, bullying 'presences' that I could understand without really hearing.

I wasn't supposed to go home but back to UCLA. There were other things I was still supposed to learn today. The lesson wasn't finished. There was a sense of homicidal nervous energy in the figures that had begun to assume shape all around me, paws and jaws, loins, eyes, the air filled with restless growls and snarls.

"Listen," I said when she answered the phone, "I have to drive out to UCLA again. I was out there this afternoon …"

"What about your classes?"

"I missed my afternoon class. Erlandson was sitting there waiting for me. Someone must have gone and told him."

"I don't know what I can do about it. I'd like to be married to a normal man. But you, I don't know, you think that I don't know anything about what is happening with you and your girlfriend? Do you think you can fool me with stories about UCLA?"

"*Te juro* … I swear," I answered, "it has nothing to do with girlfriends."

"Ever since we were in Peru. Something to do with that old Indian. Maybe you're possessed … *brujerias* … witchcraft … I'll be honest with you, I think our marriage is in serious trouble."

The 'presences' around me were becoming crazier and crazier, enormous shapes filling up the whole room, a clawed paw sweeping toward me with very real looking claws emerging from a matrix of what looked like foamy cloud.

"I've got to go," I said, hung up, and walked out to my car.

Of course she must have called Erlandson too. And I suppose Frank Sullivan had also talked to him.

Von der Ahe, Lucia, Sullivan.

I headed out to the Harbor Freeway as the voices slowly began to fill the car: *You see but a part, as far as you go, only a fraction of what you must know, great changes approaching the world around you, to us alone now you must be true …*

I parked, hungry, wanting to get a muffin and coffee. Something. But I wasn't allowed, was pushed back into the library, back to the file of *The Journal of American Folklore*, Vol.21, April-September 1908, Robert H. Lowie's "The Test-Theme in North American Mythology."

I felt myself being forced to read, the ideas being forced inside me. I wanted to rebel against all this mind-battering psychological brutality, but finally decided on the Zen solution instead and made myself passive once again, read, drank the material in, trying to understand. The article was about the same material that I had begun to view as the story of the two-twins going to the House of the Sun. Only Lowie didn't see the hidden twin-motif that I had discovered. And it was true that the way he saw it was just as valid as my vision of the story. The hero does arrive at the land on the other side of the ocean and then is tested. Jason has to kill the dragon in order to get the fleece/apples. The twins in the Hopi myth are stuck into an oven by Sun when he finally finds them. They are stuck in the oven and "cooked" – and they come out dancing. Obviously they aren't merely Venus-symbols here, but metal-symbols, tin and copper, perhaps, the ingredients of bronze. That's why the tin at Tiawanaku was so important for the ancients – it was the primary ingredient of bronze during the Bronze Age!

But I was missing the point. The demons inside my head were getting angry again, only this time they weren't surrounding me outside, in the library itself, but inside my head.

"I don't get it!" I finally growled back and shoved the volume back into its place on the shelf, and just as I reshelved it, I *did* understand – I had been reading about the Japanese myth of Ohonamuji going on a quest to marry the daughter of Susanowo ... an ancient Shinto myth from Japanese pre-history.

And suddenly I realized that the myth of Ohonamuji was a variant of *The Argonautica*. So Tiawanaku wasn't merely 'known' in the ancient Middle East/Mediterranean/Turkey. Turkey was important here. Turkey is also known as Asia Minor and Anatolia, the ultimate source for most Greek myths, the ultimate source for *The Odyssey* and *Argonautica*. But Tiawanaku was also known in Japan.

How could it be?

Was Tiawanaku the Home of the Gods, the World-Centre, the Home of the SunGods, the Solstice-Point for ancient *world* myth?

I suddenly realized that I had discovered what no one else in the world (except, perhaps, the phantom jaguars that inhabited my soul) had the slightest hint of – that the palaces and pyramids at Tiawanaku on the shore of Lake Titicaca in Bolivia, was the myth centre of *all* ancient myth, *the most important place in the ancient consciousness throughout the world!*

I stood there in the stacks at UCLA with tears streaming down my face.

Who could I tell this to? I had confided in Erlandson and he'd honestly thought I was either crazy or simply stupid; and he was one of the most sagacious people I'd ever met, his knowledge of ancient history especially vast and thorough.

I went into the rest room and washed my face, tried to calm down, wanted to be as invisible and ordinary as possible instead of looking like a bomb about to explode. Went out to my car and drove down to Malibu again, sat on the beach waiting for dark, a few swimmers and surfers, a few walkers while there was still light, but once it was dark the whole beach became almost preternaturally deserted again. Of course there was lots of crime – the last thing I was afraid of. I wasn't afraid of anything Out There, only of the 'forces' that surged and boiled inside my own head. Only tonight I was either going to have my final confrontation with them (and *triumph!*) or else I intended to strip down and swim out as far as I could and either be met by sharks like the ones I'd seen from time to time when I used to skin-dive with my students down by Palos Verdes before my trip to Peru, or else just sink from exhaustion, a few horrible moments of breathing water instead of air, but it wouldnt/couldn't really take that long ... a few moments and then peace. One thing for sure – I could not take the sort of demonic possession I was going through for one day more.

I stretched out on the sand. It was cold but I hardly felt the cold any more, like the Tibetan yogi who could regulate their temperatures at will. Or like the Dalai Lama who, before he died, said "I will never stiffen up after I die ... I can control rigor mortis too ..." And he never stiffened up after he died, had total control of his body, even after death. But to what avail if he couldn't control Death itself?

I meditated, slept, meditated some more, like taking an elevator up and down through the various levels of my soul, blissfully empty of demons, until at about midnight the demon 'presences' beginning to start to appear again, at first wispy and in the distance, but then taking form, whirling around in my head in some sort of demonic 'dance.' I remained motionless and silent until the Chief Jaguar appeared, the most gigantic of all jaguars, upright walking on his hind feet. I waited until he became aware of what I was thinking, until our minds melded and blended and he was as fully inside my despair as I myself was.

"So what do you want?" he asked, his eyes blazing, raising his left paw and silencing the others who suddenly were not merely silent, but began to dissolve altogether, back off into black distances that stretched out to infinity inside me.

"First of all, I want you to come out! Come out here so I can really see and confront you!"

"Confrontations can be fatal!" he growl-talked.

"Do you think I'm afraid of death now?" I laughed. "I'd welcome it. To be *nothing* is better than to be what I have become ..."

And I meant it. My job, my marriage ... I had hardly seen my children since all this began. Lucia had had to practically do it all, and as a scholar she was great, but being a mother as well ...

"All right," said the monster-jaguar inside my head, "space and time mean nothing to me, except perhaps as obstacles to be toyed with and overcome ..."

And in a sudden whoosh, like opening up a warm can of Pepsi, he was there in front of me, a gigantic black-yellow presence in the waning moonlight.

"So, what do you want?" asked the jaguar-master, towering above me.

"I want my life back!" I answered. "It's very simple."

Which seemed to greatly anger him.

"What do you mean, you have your life and so much more right now. You participate fully in the Spirit World, Reality as it is ..."

"Too much 'reality.' I want you and the others out of my head and life."

I was insistent and strong. There was no backing down now. I was fighting, if not for my life itself, certainly for my sanity.

"But how can I leave you now?" the giant jaguar said, slowly changing form, shrinking down, like a slide on a penny-whistle, down, down, down, down ... and I didn't know who/what was there in front of me, a beautiful young woman with long, loose black hair somewhat covering her nakedness, but not her breasts, which stuck out through the hair, nor her legs and between her legs, "*tu me dejaste despues de recibir el regalo de la vida eterna de mis manos* – you left me after having received the gift of eternal life from my hands."

Of course, now I knew who it was, Teresa – but a Teresa such as I never could have imagined had ever existed. And she was right – I even had the offers from Uncle Mario to stay in Peru with Teresa. What was I afraid of? Was it Eternal Life itself? Immortality? Was my own private deathwish so strong inside me that I could not continue to accept immortality from her hands? Because that was what she had implicitly promised me, wasn't it? Then, and again now ... reaching out, her hands full of wafers. "*Toma!* Come! Take! Eat!"

I reached out and took the wafers and stuck them in my shirt pocket and then reached out again, my fingers closed around her wrists. I wanted her there and then.

There was no Past nor Future for me at that moment, only an expanded flowering Now that I wanted to step into and never leave. Only as my fingers closed around her wrists, the wrists themselves – how shall I put it, 'dematerialised,' and I was left standing there alone in the moonlight. And I mean really *alone*, my head empty now, the 'presences' gone. There was just me, myself and I standing there in a redundancy of emptiness and I never had even come close to touching such a true sense of despair.

Had any of it really happened or was it all merely some mad drama that had played itself out on the stage of my chaotic mind? I reached into my shirt pocket and ... yes ... the wafers were there.

In a way I was free of my 'ghosts' now, back to a normality that seemed more abnormal to me than any of the mind-dramas that I had just been through. 'Normality' seemed shrunken and mean, reduced, flat, boring. In a way I wanted the jaguars back in my head, especially the towering 'chief' jaguar now that I knew it was Teresa escaped from Time, living forever on the plateau of immortality.

But I still didn't eat the wafers, instead put them in a little carved wooden box from Tegucigalpa, Honduras, that I had bought years before. A interesting little box with the stepped year-symbol on it that seemed so much more familiar to me now:

I locked it, put it in the bottom drawer of my desk and a very different epoch in my life began.

True, I was free of my 'spirits,' but on a flat, secular level I was interested in nothing else but the ancient so-called New World.

The next day I took Lucia and the kids down to Chinatown in downtown L.A., a place where none of my colleagues went. To them Los Angeles was Westchester, maybe the area around USC, Westwood (UCLA), but downtown (including Chinatown and Little Tokyo) was totally off limits.

But if Los Angeles was a wild, third world city, so be it. Let me enjoy it a little, now that my ghosts were gone.

On the way home, the three kids in the back seat of the car asleep, Lucia asked me.

"You seem like a different person tonight. I even wanted to take a picture. Your whole face is different. Did you break up with her?"

"I tried to grab her arm, but she dematerialised," I answered. That was what had happened, hadn't it? Couldn't I simply state my truths the way they had happened to me?

"I'm sure she did, eventually they always do," said Lucia and reached over and turned on the radio, which I always had tuned to Pacifica Radio. Mahler's 9th Symphony, the fourth movement, both the best and the worst music for the moment. It must have been the Bernstein recordings, getting every last drop of pathos out of it.

What was the best way to describe it, discordant schmaltz, music to be played during the last scene of the end of the world.

I couldn't help myself, started to cry again, Lucia, of course, picking up on it, totally misinterpreting it.

"She must have meant a lot to you."

I reached down and turned off the radio, opened the window a little and refused to answer her, which I suppose was the real answer that she wanted anyhow.

The next day I started work on my Henry James book again. I was dealing with the late novels now, *The Golden Bowl*, *The Ambassadors* ... and I loved James' message – to grab on to life, no matter what form it took, to grab on to it. Although it was exactly the opposite of what I had done. By refusing to take the wafers that Teresa had given me, I had guaranteed my own death, hadn't I? Plus the loss of all the powers that I was obviously beginning to acquire, the powers that she had so totally dominated and used – shape-changing, spirit-travel, the ability to 'spiritualise,' then 'reconcretise' – things that we usually only associate with the soul after death. If then. Call them 'ghosts-powers.' Could I, I wondered, have been able to travel into her world the way she had travelled into mine? Could I have simultaneously lived in Los Angeles and in the Madre de Dios jungle, lived inside her head the way she had lived inside mine?

I began to spend more time with the kids in the afternoons.

Erlandson even came into my office one afternoon while I was sitting there reading *The Ambassadors*, taking notes.

"I'm glad to see you back with us. And, to be honest with you, I'm curious as hell to know exactly what you were going through ..."

"Oh, some kind of virus, I suppose," I lied.

Why should I tell the truth. All he would do is scoff and I didn't need that right now in the midst of all the spiritual emptiness I was feeling, my own private *noche oscuro del alma*, dark night of the soul, which is the way San Juan de la Cruz, the Spanish mystic, describes his feelings of deprivation of the Divine Presence. I couldn't help but wonder what mushrooms or cacti, moulds or even the natural imbalances of his own personal chemical makeup he had experienced to trigger off these images in his poetry ...

Everything was 'normal,' but at the same time every night I found myself obsessively involved with reading everything I could find about the Pre-Columbian world. At first I totally believed that Teresa and her friends were gone forever from my life, but slowly, as I uncovered more and more links between the Old and New Worlds in ancient times, I began to suspect that she was still there guiding me. Invisible and inaudible, but still somehow *there*.

How else could I have so adroitly and unerringly come across books like Vincent Fidel Lopez's *Races Aryennes du Perou*, written by a Bolivian and published in Paris in 1871. It was a book that should have totally changed the nature of ancient history, but no book had been more carefully ignored. By whom? And why?

Lopez, a hundred years earlier, had noticed that Quechua, the language of the Incas, was essentially the same as Sanskrit, one of the basic languages of ancient India. His book is filled with endless lists comparing the two languages:

	QUECHUA	SANSKRIT
MOON	Paksha	Paksa
VASE	Sunu	Suna
MOUTH/SMILE	Simi (mouth)	Simi (smile)
THORN	Tankat	Tank
MOON/WHITE/SHINING	Killa (moon)	Kil (white/shining)

Which, of course, meant that the Quechua-speakers in the Andes were somehow connected with ancient India. I came across references in Thor Heyerdahl's *Ancient Man and the Sea* that talked about how the Spaniards had noticed that the inhabitants around Lake Titicaca area in Peru were lighter than themselves. And the Incas always traced their origins back to Lake Titicaca, right next to Tiawanaku. Inca legend said that the Sun had descended on an island in the middle of Lake Titicaca that was called the Island of the Sun, and that from the Sun had emerged the first Inca couple, the progenitors of the whole Inca race. Which agreed, didn't it, with the whole idea that Lake Titicaca/Tiawanaku was the Land of the Sun-King?

And weren't the Incas simply saying that they were the descendents of the original rulers of Tiawanaku?

I discovered that Tiawanaku had been destroyed by floods and earthquakes. At least that's what Posnansky says in his *Tihuanacu – The Cradle of American Man*. Posnansky had spent much of his life at Tiawanaku (Tihuanacu) and in excavating the ruins he found them under a huge amount of alluvium, dirt that he felt had been washed down over the ruins in ancient times when earthquakes had broken open the basins of lakes that lie above Tiawanaku, inundating the buildings with flood-waters.

In another much ignored book, *America's Ancient Civilizations* (1953), A.H. and R. Verrill don't talk about Sanskrit-Quechua connections, but connections between Quechua and Sumerian ... and I slowly began to see how Sanskrit, Sumerian and Quechua, in a sense, are all part of the same linguistic-cultural group ... like in the word NAKU, which forms part of the name of the place itself.

It means serpent and is *naga* in Sanskrit, *naku* in Sumerian, *nakash* in Hebrew.

In fact the name is written on the ruins itself, something that I was the first one to notice. Written in letters/glyphs taken from the ancient Middle East/India. There are essentially three letters:

◯ = TI   〰〰 = A   ⌐┐ = NAKU

Only they aren't written exactly in this way. The sun-glyph (TI) is written surrounded by the water glyph (A) in one pictographic-alphabetic complex:

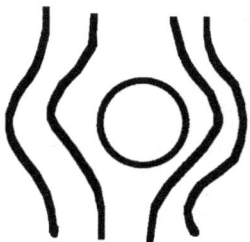

More or less the way South America is surrounded by water – the sun/Land of the Sun-King/The Solstice Point surrounded by water. And the Naku is written just like in the old Middle Eastern/Indus alphabets. In fact it was when I was in the midst of decoding all the letters that up to this time had been considered just "decorations" on the ruins at Tiawanaku, that I had shown it to my old Kabbalist friend, Menke Katz, and he had turned the symbol on its side and identified it as *nakash*, the Hebrew equivalent of *naku* (Sumerian), the Sanskrit *naga*. What did this tell me? That I was home! It was all true, the links were there.

I remember another day, somehow I found myself with a copy of Dick Ibarra Grasso's *La Escritura Indígena Andina – Indigenous Andean Writing* in my hands, a book about a writing-system that the Spaniards had found the natives in the Andes using when they had first arrived there in the sixteenth century.

Just the week before somehow I had been reading through Volume II of Sir John Marshall's *Mohenjodaro and the Indus Civilization*, the great mother-civilisation of India, looking through page after page of the still undeciphered Indus Valley inscriptions/alphabet. And suddenly, it was like a spark-machine ... the connection was made and the stuttering blue current began to go mad.

They were the same letters. Very, very slight variations!

Indus Valley Script in the Andes	*Indus Valley Script in India*
ᘳ	ᘯ
◊	◊
ᨆ	ᨆ
ᨇ	ᨇ
ᨈ	ᨈ

And in Marshall's book on the Indus Valley he had charts that showed the links between Indus Valley and Sumerian letters. So not only the languages (Naku/Naga) linked up together, but also the letters.

The original settlers in the Andes, the builders of Tiawanaku, were originally from India-Iraq!

They were all part of the same family. You could see it everywhere. Take a word like the Quechua *Apu* for Lord, the name they used to designate the Inca emperor – *Apu Inca*, Lord Inca. *Apu* was Quechua, exactly the same as the Sumerian *Apu*, like the Assyrian-Akkadian *Abu*, the somewhat more distant Hebrew *Abba*. Take a word like the Quechua word for Sister: *Ahua/Ahualla*. In Assyrian and Akkadian it was *Ahatu*, in Hebrew *Ahote*.

The strangest thing was that in Sumerian myth the inhabitants of Anaku, the Annunaki, were considered the elder gods ... as if ... as if the great civilization had *begun* in the Andes and only then moved to India/The Middle East.

I became totally obsessed with my work. I could hardly think about anything else. My Freshman comp classes became classes about ancient archaeology, alphabets, languages. I started comparing the drain-systems at Tiawanaku and the drain-systems in Mohenjo-Daro in what is today Pakistan, one of the most important of the Indus Valley civilisation cities. They were almost exactly the same. My students, instead of writing about "What I did last summer," or "Projections – Me in Fifty Years, What Will My Life Have Been Like?" were writing about comparative drain-systems in the Indus Valley and ancient Tiawanaku, about the similarities between Hindu Siva figures as starving yoga, and similar figures from Tiawanaku, Easter Island and Mohenjo Daro.

Years earlier, when the Indus Valley civilisation had been first unearthed, a scholar named Guillaume de Hevesy had noticed the similarities between the alphabet used by the "natives" on Easter Island, and the Indus Valley alphabet, drawing a direct line between Easter Island, off the coast of Chile in the South Pacific, and ancient India. Now what I had done was to draw the line up into the Andes.

In fact another scholar, Thor Heyerdahl, proved that there was a direct link between the earliest sculpture at Tiawanaku and the earliest sculpture on Easter Island ... and when I discovered that the first settlers on Easter Island were called the Miru, my head went wild again.

Of course! Tiawanaku was the home of the gods in ancient world myth! What about in India where the centre of sacred geography is Mount Meru! The Miru from Tiawanaku were the first settlers on Easter Island.

IMMORTAL JAGUAR

Siva as lord of Yoga – the Master of Asceticism

Siva at Tiawanaku

Siva from Easter Island

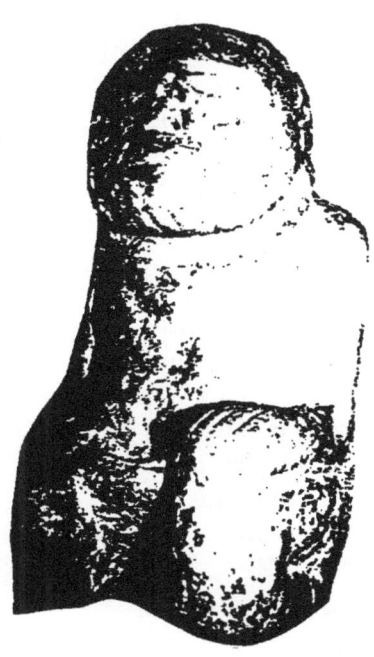

Siva from Mohenjo Daro

The Miru come from Meru. Why hadn't I seen it before – Tiawanaku was also the centre of Hindu sacred geography.

I looked very carefully at the geographical structure of Hindu sacred geography. It was broken down into quarters and each quarter had its own "god," Indra in the East, Varuna in the West, Kubera in the North, Yama in the South.

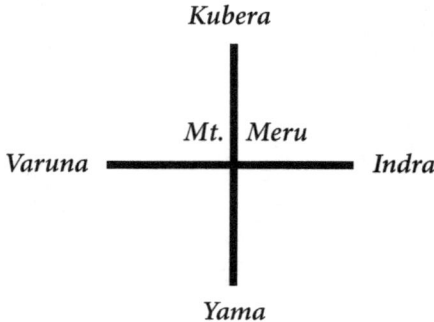

And if I placed this 'system' on the actual mythic geography of ancient Peru–Bolivia, all the gods fell suddenly into place.

If I went west from Tiawanaku to the world of Varuna I suddenly came face to face with one of the most famous oracles from pre-Columbian times – the oracle at Pachacamac. Varuna is a kind of weather-forcaster, a god of the sea. Which is exactly the same as the oracle at Pachacamac. To the east of Mount Meru is Mount Illimani whose name is derived from an ancient Andean ILLA-root concerned with thunder and lightning: Illapu (lightning, thunder). Indra is intimately connected with thunder, lightning, storms.

Kubera is the god of dwarfs, associated with precious metals and mining. The Bolivian high plain is filled with stories about dwarf-miners called Ekkekos. One day years before, I had been having lunch at the house of one of Mariano Baptista's sisters, and her son had brought out a small, perfect little ceramic statue of a hunchbacked figure, asked me "What do you think about this?"

"It's an Ekkeko, right?" I answered.

Hunchbacked, with the sun and copulating snakes symbols on it:

TI   NAKU

So I guess I knew where the figure had come from!

Another day I saw a black dwarf mummy in the museum of the Catholic University in Sucre, Bolivia – with its heart torn out.

One day in the Maya Book of Chilam Balaam [the Jaguar Priest] of Chumayel, I came across the name Ah Yamas as the god of the South. It was hard to believe. It was almost exactly the same as the Hindu god of the South, Yama ... the Lord of the Underworld. Among the southwest Sia Indians another day I came across the god of the South as Yuma. Not Yama but Yuma. Yuma, Yama, Ah Yamas. And there *was* a ruin in Peru that was very suggestive of being related to Yama, the bull-headed god in Hindu mythology – Chavín de Huantar – with its strange, diabolical images of a multiheaded god half bull, half jaguar, whose image can be viewed either rightside up or upside down, who carries a trident and whose image is filled with serpents:

 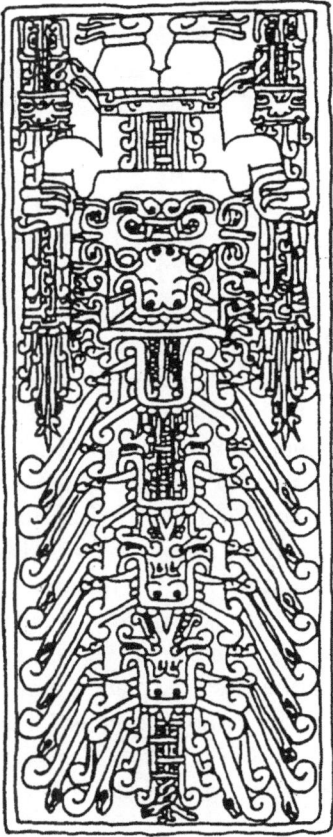

What I still hadn't found out about was the entrance to the caves under the Andes at the base of Mount Illimani, and the legends about a bull-headed god who emerges from the underworld every spring!

Yama, the bull-headed god of the Underworld in India. A bull-headed god who emerges from a cave-world under the Andes every spring. An exact match.

So in the course of immersing myself totally in ancient New and Old World myth, anthropology, archaeology and art, I had stumbled upon yet another link between the Andes and ancient India.

Pachacamac = Varuna
Illimani = Indra
The dwarf miners in the Andes = Kubera
Yama = The Lord of the Underworld located under the Andes.

And in the course of unearthing these connections, I slowly became aware of the great quantity of research that had already been done (all covered up, ignored, ridiculed by The Academic Establishment!) linking the ancient Chinese, Japanese, Sumerians and other Middle Easterners to the New World. I was the first to arrive at a total, coherent overview, but there were all sorts of other scholars who were unearthing the same kinds of connections. In 1955 Carl Hentze had had a book published in German in Zürich called *Das mythische Bild* (mythical picture) *in ältesten China* (in ancient China) *in der Grossasiatischen und Zircumpazifischen Kulturen* (in the major Asiatic and circum-Pacific cultures). My German served me well. I discovered the work of Robert Heine-Geldern, materials that were coming out just as I was making my own discoveries. Like the article in the *Handbook of Middle American Indians* (1966) on "The Problem of Transpacific Influences in Mesoamerica."

It turned out that in Chinese myth there was a similar picture of a central mountain, Mount Kunlun ... again Tiawanaku.

Everywhere I looked it was always the same.

I remember reading through the whole file of the Polynesian Society Memoiries (sic) from New Zealand and coming across (in Volume III, 1913) a whole article on "The Lore of the Whare Wananga," an ancestral home in the west, the place where the god Tane brought down knowledge from the uppermost heavens. Of course Whare Wananga was Tiawanaku.

WHARE   WANANGA
TIA   WANAKU

And the god "Tane," who I kept coming across in my readings on South Sea myth and anthropology, was known variously as Tane, Kane, Con ... which checked with one of the names of Viracocha, the god who had brought civilisation to the Andes.

Tane is described as having a human head and a snake's body.

Which, of course, is the same as the description of Quetzalcoatl in Mexican myth, Quetzalcoatl, the Plumed-Serpent, with a human head and snake's body. And Quetzalcoatl was the great civiliser in Mexico, the same as Tane-Kane-Con-Viracocha in the South Seas and Bolivia. The equivalent in Egyptian myth is Osiris.

Quetzalcoatl leaves Central America in a raft made of serpents.

Osiris lives in a house in the sea with walls of living serpents.

The land of the gods in Egyptian myth is Ta-Neteru:

TA — NETERU
TIA—WANAKU

What I had obviously uncovered was:
1. The fact that in world myth there was a home of the gods associated with psychedelic plants that made man immortal,
2. That this place under various names was really Tiawanaku/Anaku.

Behind all the myths was a real place and real drugs ... and real immortals.

All the linguistics, archaeology and anthropology matched up with the myths.

The people in the Andes were speaking languages related to the languages of the ancient Middle East and India. They had an alphabet that was the same as the alphabet of the Indus Valley civilisation in ancient India. The name Tiawanaku was written on the ruins themselves as TI-A-NAKU using ancient Middle Eastern/Indus letters.

Only the fact that Quechua and Sanskrit were the same was uncovered at the end of the nineteenth century. The similarities between Quechua and Sumerian had been known for years. How could the "orthodox" view that the New World had been exclusively inhabited across the Bering Strait during the Ice Age hold up? But that was what was being taught everywhere, not as theory but absolute fact.

I found myself in the eerie position of being the first person to see it all the way it really was, to understand that the myth of the hero going across the ocean to the Home of the Gods/Land of the Sun King/The Tin Lands was really an astronomical-celestial cryptogram encoding in itself the voyage of the sun through the zodiac which also served as a star chart to bring ancient mariners to the New World, and that this Home of the Gods wasn't fantasy but a real place on the shores of Lake Titicaca in Bolivia. And behind the myths of the Egyptian Osiris, the Mexican Quetzalcoatl, the South Seas Kane-Tane and the Andean Viracocha-Con was a real "god-man" who had travelled across the Atlantic (and Pacific?) in ancient times …

The Chinese knew about The New World and travelled there. So did the Japanese, the ancient Indians in India, ancient New Zealanders, the "Turks" from whom the Greeks had derived their myths about Helios, the Sun-God.

The God-Kings were real people, the Home of the Gods was a real place … and the immortality spoken of in the myths seemed just as real to me after all the experiences I had been through.

I had been touched by one of the immortals and when I had reached out to touch her back, she had dissolved in my hand.

As time went on I became more and more alienated from my wife. I moved out into the garage of our little house on Jenny street, nailed the garage-door shut and lined the walls with bookcases.

I didn't go out at night any more but would spend my nights either in my new workroom or at the library at Loyola or UCLA.

I found it increasingly difficult to teach my classes in American Literature.

Melville, Thoreau and Emerson meant nothing to me any more. I was only interested in one thing – the reality behind the legends of The Immortals.

And I longed to return to Peru, to Uncle Mario's *hacienda*. But Lucia refused to go with me. Whatever had happened to me had happened there, and she found it a lot easier to deal with me as the fanatic scholar I had become than the possessed jaguar shaman that I had been.

Then she got me invited to the last great poetry pow wow of the 60s held at Berkeley in April of 1968. Some friend of hers at San Fernando State University. I went and read some of my poetry. Which didn't sound so much like poetry as poeticised anthropology:

> seven word
> worlds
> stages
> seven

winter death-life
rungs
out of
Samsara/isolation
illusion
into
communal yogic
spring
self into
sacred lightning
snake
eagle
rain cloud
terraces ...
Hitkasharu
H'Atira
(Kawas)
cloud-eagle-snake
descends
I become Snake Mother.
(from *Oma*, excerpted from *Obras*, Vol.12 No.1, Spring 1981, pp.24-25)

My work was well received, and I began to somehow identify all the myths surrounding the ancient Home of the Gods with the Hippy Movement that was just emerging out of its Beat beginnings.

The Beats had still been occidental for all their strivings toward orientalisation. They had laid the theoretical foundations for the Hippy Movement, but the Hippies were moving into a whole new sphere of experiential existentialism where occidental pragmatism and scientism was being transmuted into buddhistic-yogic contemplativeness. The Western World was being turned into a celebration of existence. I honestly expected some sort of New Millennium to take place, a shift of consciousness away from money-grubbing and war into a triumph of aesthetics and love. It was all guitars and long hair, flowers and flowered clothes, pot and mushrooms, a smiling rush into an Augmented Now ...

I remember spending endless hours in the chapel at Loyola-Marymount between classes, or walking along the bluff that looked out on the Los Angeles Basin, with the big sign HOLLYWOOD in the far distance that you could only see on smogless days after a rain, thinking about the New Millennium that I believed was in its birth throes. And, of course, my thoughts went back to what I knew about The Immortals – that there was a place in South America that in worldwide ancient myth was known as the Home of the Gods, where the gods lived and ate "apples" that made them immortal and where ordinary mortals like myself, when we ate these same apples, *became* immortal, turned into jaguar shamans and became godlike ourselves …

I would sit in the back of the colonial Spanish chapel, my thoughts going something like this:

> … Immortality makes sense, doesn't it? Everywhere you look there is evidence of The Divine. Look at the intestinal tract, all the enzymes and juices, the gallbladder, gall itself, the nerves and muscles, every bug and plant, a newborn kitten. The Creator is everywhere imprinted on His-Her Creation. And how can we have been created to simply 'die'? There has to be immortality. Only is it the spirit going off to some sort of Never-Never-Land Heaven, or immortality on Earth? The pilgrimages of the ancients were always to the same place – Tiawanaku. Had the gods from Tiawanaku finally died … or had they moved elsewhere? Were they 'in hiding?' And was the whole Hippy Movement that was coming alive around me somehow connected with the ancient gods? Were all the beads and flowers and consciousness-altering drugs the heralds of universalisation of the Tiawanakan Mystique? When the Huichol Indians in northern Mexico took their sacred Peyote, they believed that they died and passed through the vaginal gates of rebirth which was what the clashing gates motif was all about in ancient Greek myth. They died and were reborn and entered into the ancestral lands of Wirakuta which was the Land of Viracocha, the name given to the Sun-God Culture-Hero of Tiawanaku … so everything went back to Tiawanaku … even the Garden of Eden in the bible was a reference to Tiawanaku … the immortals/the gods couldn't have died, they must have gone elsewhere. Only where? There was some sort of cryptogram that I had to decode. That was my place in the holy scheme of things – to somehow link The Ancient and the Future, tie together The Hippy Revolution and the Jaguar Shamanism of the Immortals of the Ancient Past …

I didn't feel comfortable at Loyola-Marymount any more and started looking around for a job elsewhere, somewhere religiously 'neutral.' Which was how I happened to move to Michigan and got a job teaching in the department of American Thought and Language at Michigan State.

In 1968 I met Charles Bukowski, kind of the King of the Literary Rebels of the 1960s, an aging postal clerk-poet-novelist who thumbed his nose at everything bourgeoisie and 'normal'. I wrote a critical-bibliographical study of Bukowski, then a book on another poet, Lyn Lifshin, yet another on Charles Potts, started a little poetry magazine of my own, *Ghost Dance*. For a while seemed almost severed from my deep, existential ties with Tiawanaku/South America.

Lucia and I got divorced. I had a 'reader' in the Department of American Thought and Language, a young married graduate student from Kansas. We fell in love, both of us got divorced and we got married and immediately started having kids.

If you would have come to Michigan and seen me at the beginning of the 1970s, married, living in this old 1904 house with the oak trimmed interiors, the father of two little girls, putting together a critical book and poetry anthology on the new Hippy writers (books that eventually came out as *The Living Underground – A Critical Overview* and *The Living Underground – A Poetry Anthology*) you would have thought I had completely severed my ties with the The Ancients and all the revelations that I had had about the Home of the Gods.

Only then one fine Autumn day I was wandering through the Beal Botanical Gardens on the campus at Michigan State and one of the signs on one of the plants caught my attention:

JIMSON WEED – AMERICAN DATURA.

So-called from "Jamestown," where it was grown. a Native American hallucinogenic plant.

I immediately remembered a Hopi tale called "The Jimson Weed Girls." Which goes something like this … a young man one day walked into the tribe of Jimson Weed Girls and had sex with every one of them until he was having sex with the final girl, who had a toothed-vagina (*vagina dentada*) and cut off his penis.

I looked carefully at the seed-pods on the plants. They were vagina-shaped, with "teeth" along the entire edge:

When I had first read the story twenty years earlier I didn't have a hint as to what it meant, but now suddenly I understood it all. There were no Jimson Weed Girls, of course, but there was the Jimson Weed itself. If you took a lot of it you were rendered impotent.

It was a perfect example of the radical metaphor-making of the Proto-Historic Imagination – like turning the sun's journey through the year into the hero's journeys across the ocean through a myriad of adventures that were ultimately based on a journey through the zodiac.

How complicated/complex can you get? You choose the constellation that appears in the sky above the place where the sun has set and make that into your zodiac sign. Say that at a given moment in the solar year the sign above the setting sun is Leo/The Knife/Flint … then you create a story about the sun (or the twins/Venus) conquering/killing a Lion … or, as in the Hopi story, killing a Flint-Monster.

Now here was the transformation of a plant into a tribe of women who cut off the penis of a man who had sex with them.

When I first read the sign I was with my two little girls, Margaret and Alexandra, so I took them home, and then that night, without saying anything to my wife, I got up in the middle of the night, the voices already beginning in my head "We want you back, you are one of us now, forever and forever, you must return, you must not die," and I went back to the gardens, harvested a pocketful of the seedpods, intending to go home and try them out there, but it was as if I were losing control again, as if my hand wasn't mine, but being controlled by "Them" ("Her"), and there, right in the middle of the garden, surrounded by the strangest, most bizarre plants in the world, the entire campus one vast botanical museum that, I suppose, called up Amazonia inside me, a thousand Amazonias, right there next to the carp pond, under the Mother of All Willows. I started chewing on the seeds, felt my throat clamp shut but instead of stopping chewing, continued on, feeling my arms and legs start to tighten up, gasping for breath, falling down, still chewing, the voices urging me on, "You must go through the gates of rebirth, die in order to be reborn again," presences slowly beginning to materialise around me, the air filled with the pungent, musky smell of the great cats, jaguar-tiger people huddling around me again, then the Master Jaguar, the great giant among them, approaching me, stepping behind me as I felt mucous begin to stream out of my nose and mouth like thick strings.

"At last you return to me," it (she) said. And it was as if I were hearing two voices. Or the same voice on two levels. On one level was the growling, guttural jaguar voice, but on the other the voice of the old/eternally-young woman, Doña Teresa-Teresita. "It has been such a long time ... I finally brought you here so you come to me through the door of the gods ..."

Feeling myself fall down on the grass as she reached down and ripped her enormous paw across my throat, feeling the blood spurting out again all over me in a sudden wet rush of warmth, and then ZERO again, NON-NESS ...

When I woke up, the sky was just beginning to turn light, the Morning Star above the just-about-to-emerge sun ... and I understood for the first time the passage in the Maya Popul Vuh about the Old Sun dying and the Morning Star, Hun-Hunapu, the Little Lord, actually *becoming* the New Sun, all that equivalence between Morning Star and Sun ...

It was the day of the Autumnal Equinox.

Of course! That was why I had been brought to this place at this moment. We were at one of the key points in the configuration of the solar year.

I was shivering. It must have been in the upper forties. My shirt was soaked with sweat, my nose streaming with mucous. The campus was still pretty much dead so I got up and hurried home, showered, changed clothes, looked in the mirror and what looked back out at me was a wild-eyed jaguar, my head filled again with a backdrop of rolling, unfurling continuous growls.

The possession had begun again. I went back into my bedroom and slept for a while, and then about nine, Nona, my wife, came in with coffee.

"Did I hear you go out last night and then come in again just before dawn?"

"You did ..." I went into my coat pocket and pulled out the seed-pods, spread them out on the bed. "These are datura seed-pods. They are 'keys' into the Other World. I first saw them yesterday afternoon, went back last night, chewed on some seeds and went through another death-resurrection ritual. My jaguar-self is back."

"Why didn't you take me with you?" she said, reaching down for the seeds.

"No, it's very dangerous," I said, grabbing the pods, shoving them back in my pocket.

Of course I was afraid of what Teresa might do to her if she should ever get her alone in the Spirit World.

"Nothing is too dangerous for me whenever you're concerned," said Nona, reaching into my pocket.

But I wouldn't let her get near the seeds, got up and went outside into the backyard and scattered them to the winds, little realising that sowing seeds doesn't get rid of them but produces crops the following year, and that Datura is an especially persistent, tough 'predator' to get rid of.

The result of this one episode of self-indulgence was that I was totally possessed again by the jaguar presences.

I remember going over to the Michigan State University library and getting a carrel, a little 'office' of sorts up on the third floor in the front, looking out on the campus, right in the middle of the trees. In fact it had the feeling of a tree-house about it. And I would spend *most* of my time there.

I continued to immerse myself in ancient cultures in both the New and Old Worlds and uncover more and more links between ancient China, Japan, Africa, the Middle East and India and the New World. I was never free of the persistent, humming presence of my jaguar masters. I was being 'guided.' I was the Chosen One, chosen to put all the links together into some sort of coherent whole.

Things happened that seemed just coincidence, but at the same time they seemed to always be 'guided,' and part of larger, planned structures.

For some years I had been a pen pal of a guy named Jerry Dombrowski in Boston. I'd submitted a short play and some poetry to his magazine *Abyss* while I was still at Loyola-Marymount, and when I'd spent the summer of 1968 in Providence, Rhode Island at Brown University on a Brown University Library grant, I'd gone up to Boston and visited Dombrowski and we'd become great friends.

He was in the process of bringing out a book of essays about a far-out contemporary philosopher named John Brockman, and Jerry asked me "Would you like to contribute to the volume?"

Strangely enough, the 'vectors,' the 'forces' inside me encouraged me to somehow link up with Brockman. It was strange how I always knew what I should or shouldn't do. If I embarked on some project unrelated to the purposes of the jaguar-shaman world, my whole inner being would go beserk, and I would be filled with stinging, lacerating waves of "mind-agony." That's the best way to describe it – waves of mental agony. But when I did what They wanted, then I would be filled with a sense of buoyant joy.

Which was the way I felt working on the Brockman essay.

I wondered, in fact, whether Brockman was part of some sort of deep philosophical change that the Invisible World was effecting on the Visible World. Did the Immortals (which was the way I now saw them) have some sort of plan for restoring their hegemony in the world? They had been the spiritual centre of the world in ancient times; now was there some sort of restoration of this centricity in the modern world, perhaps at the beginning of the next millennium?

Certainly Brockman's message was clear – all traditional views of Man as a "spiritual being" had been replaced by a new view, just beginning to come into vogue, of man as neurological "machine." When we look out at the world and think, feel, aspire, despair, there really is no 'we.' We are neurological machines, nothing more.

A radical view at best.

But, I wondered, how could Brockman possibly serve the purposes of The Immortals?

And then one day I received a letter from Brockman himself that clarified it all:

Dear Hugh,
I am about to embark on a new career as a literary agent. Do you have any books (non-fiction) that you would like to see me market?
Best,
John

I immediately wrote back that I didn't have any book written yet, but for years I had been totally immersed in the same subject, ancient New-Old World ties – would he be interested?

This was before faxes and e-mail, but he called me the moment he got my letter. Yes, he was interested. It was exactly the sort of book he wanted to market.

And that was how my book *The Gods of the Cataclysm* got written, a book that summed up all my research to that point. Brockman came through for me – *Gods* was published by Harper's Magazine Press in 1976. A second book, an anthology of Central and South American Indian poetry called *First Fire*, came out at the same time from Doubleday. I was beginning to make a little mark as an anthropologist-archaeologist.

But the ways of the Immortals are devious, and I now see that their real purpose was for me to meet a Bolivian on a plane going back to the US from Guayaquil, stopping off at Quito where the Bolivian would get on the plane and sit down next to me and tell me about the cave-world under the Andes ...

The Gods of the Cataclysm was about to come out when Von Däniken brought out his *The Gold of the Gods*. Von Däniken had already published *The Chariots of the Gods* some years earlier, a book that claims that the figures all over the ground at Nazca in Peru were designed as airport markers for ancient astronauts.

It wasn't a particularly new idea when Von Däniken wrote it. For years I had been reading *Planeta*, a magazine devoted to the development of this whole theory of the extraterrestrial origin of New World Cultures.

I even thought it made some sense. Certainly some sort of 'epiphany' seems to have occurred in both the New and Old Worlds in ancient times. The book of Ezechiel is filled with descriptions of some sort of machine that contained wheels within wheels-like a space ship. When Moses goes up to the mountain to receive the ten commandments, if you read the Hebrew very carefully you will see that 'God' doesn't allow Moses to see his face, but merely his 'backside.' There is a constant communication between 'God' and 'Man.' It happens, certain truths are revealed – and then the communication is severed. The Egyptian God, Osiris, the great civilizer who travels all over the world preaching doctrines practically identical to the Ten Commandments (against murder, for compassion, 'humanity') is obviously the same person (simply with a different name) as Viracocha in Peru, Quetzalcoatl in Mexico. In fact, if you carefully examine the names of the Sun-God/Civilizer left behind in the New World and compare them to the names of the Sun-God/Civilizer in the Old World, you can see they are the same:

NEW WORLD	**OLD WORLD**
Sua (among the Chibcha in Colombia)	Surya (Hindu)
Ra (Peru)	Ra (Egyptian)
Con (Peru)	Con/Kane/Tane (SouthSeas)
Votan (Tzendal Indians in Mexico)	Votan (German Sun-God)

(From Thor Heyerdahl's *Early Man and the Ocean*, p.109 ff.)

Only this great 'civilizer' and 'law-giver' is always presented as a god. No one says that a bearded white *man* suddenly appeared who presented a particular people with a code of laws; it is always a *god*. The same as in our bible. In fact our bible is merely one document among many that spells out this same reality – Man was 'touched' by God/The Gods in a myriad of places throughout the world. He had come to bring The Word. Was he merely a man who had been divinised by sacred drugs, or was he an extra-terrestrial and were the visitations part of a larger scheme of colonising Earth?

I'll be honest. The first draft of *The Gods of the Cataclysm* concentrated quite a bit on extra-terrestrials. The idea was everywhere. Even among the Incas. The Inca legend about their origin is quite explicit – The Sun Descended on an Island in the Middle of Lake Titicaca and out of it emerged the founders of the Inca civilisation. Of course the "sun descending" sounded like a space-ship of some sort descending. It certainly *seemed* that at some time around, say, 3,000 B.C., that the earth was visited by a moral and spiritual rescue mission from outer space.

So ... when *The Gold of the Gods* came out in 1976 and Von Däniken put some pictures in the book of gold objects that supposedly had been found in caves under the Andes and had been brought to an old priest in Cuenca, Ecuador, named Father Crespi, filled with writing that I immediately recognised as Indus Valley script which was also Andean Indigenous Script, I decided to immediately fly down to Ecuador and check it all out.

I remember calling Larry Freudlich at Harper's Magazine Press from the airport in New York. He wasn't in, but his secretary was; and she became all disturbed about my leaving.

"You can't go off into the Ecuadorian jungle now; your book is about to come out. What if something happens to you?"

"Something is definitely going to happen to me," I answered, "my jaguars are very happy ..."

"Your what?" she asked.

"Nothing," I answered, "just an old Chibcha saying – you are happy when the jaguars inside you are happy ..."

"Whatever," she answered, "so go get killed and miss all the talk shows and subsidiary rights!"

And she hung up.

I flew down to Guayaquil on the Ecuadorian coast, stayed in a *pensión* for a couple of days before taking a bus up to Cuenca.

My jaguars *were* very happy. I was somehow on the right track, and I couldn't help but wonder if the 'presences' inside me weren't the same as the presences who had made themselves known to the ancients under the names of Ra, Surya, Votan, Con? Were the Immortals about to initiate some sort of Second Coming? They had obviously come once, tried to civilise and reform Man, but had failed. Now were they about to try again?

Brockman's own writing began to take on curiously prophectic and cryptic overtones for me. I used to carry my copy of *By The Late John Brockman* (Toronto: Macmillan Company, 1969) with me everywhere I went (including Ecuador). What was I to make of statements like these?

Man is dead. We are now concerned with the concept of process ... Instead of 'man' and 'not-man,' we move the object-subject separation one step back to objectify a universe of simultaneous operations ... in this system there is "not only a universe, but there are also elements capable of observing this universe." Reality is no longer to be found hiding out in the subjects and objects of 'man' and 'not man.'
(p.35)

For discussing integration at the neural level we must look at what man called the interval, a nonexistent moment to the invisible. Man was, in a very real sense, man-made. The process was invisible.
(p.36)

What is the point of attempting to correlate patterns of neural activity to man's mind, feelings, emotions, etc.? We can dispense with these abstractions. They are from another epoch. They are of little usefulness in dealing with operant phenomena.
(p.44)

Obviously Brockman was talking about the birth of some sort of New Age here, some sort of direct neural link to Reality. Moses was not allowed to see the face of God (the jets of some sort of reactor system?) but only his "backside" (the ship itself, made into some sort of larger-than-life anthropomorphic image?) Now was Man at last going to be allowed to view God (The Gods) face to face?

I had become some sort of tool for The Gods to open up the future with. They were using my own natural scholarly inclinations in order to feed information into me that would totally transform the world, perhaps not even back to what it was, but lead it up on to some sort of new spiritual plane undreamed of in our projections and philosophies.

Little hints were being dropped for me everywhere that I barely understood.

Looking back now I realise that I was a very imperfect instrument for the changes that were in the works. I remember how completely out of it I felt when I arrived in Guayaquil. It was hot, muggy, very third-worldish, poor, disorganised, run-down. When I had been in South America with Lucia I was always at home. She was my key, my spiritual passport. But now alone, it was very different. Being married to a white woman from Kansas had begun to turn whole areas of my soul back into Señor Gringo.

I could have gone directly on to Cuenca where Padre Crespi, the old priest the Indians had supposedly been bringing objects to out of caves under the Andes, was living in a monastery and had become some sort of folk-hero, local "saint." But I stayed in Guayaquil, went to the local museum and saw some beautiful ceramics, and spent quite a bit of time talking to the owner of the *pensión* (boarding house) where I was staying. I always travelled cheap. I didn't like fancy hotels. The *vagabundo* in my soul was very happy with the most humble accommodations. And even in this, the purposes of The Immortals were silently and invisibly involved. Why that particular hotel? Why Sr. Rodriguez?

Now I can see it, but I couldn't see it then.

I got to talking with Sr. Rodriguez about Von Däniken's *The Gold of the Gods*, the whole business of Indians bringing strange art objects out of caves under the Andes, told him about how I had discovered the fact that Tiawanaku was the Home of the Gods/The World-Centre/House of the Sun in ancient world myth and how the myths themselves were cryptograms that had encoded into them a star-chart based on the zodiac that was used by ancient mariners to get to the New World ... very specifically, to Tiawanaku.

Sr. Rodriguez took a little sip of rum and coke, put up his hand and quietly said "I am from the province of Limón here in Ecuador and there are all kinds of caves there. In fact there is a network of caves that stretches throughout the Andes. You can go all the way from Ecuador to Cuzco by cave ..."

And *this* bit of information was what I had come to Guayaquil for. My jaguars knew it; there was deep rejoicing inside my soul when Rodriguez mentioned the caves, but somehow I still didn't get the big picture.

Of course I was barely surviving psychologically. The presence of ancient jaguar spirits inside me directing and guiding me ... if I had gone to any psychologist about *that*, I would have ended up in a psychiatric ward under heavy sedation taking Haldol or Clozaril. I had to maintain a calm face in spite of the band of jaguars inside me, in spite of the fact that I was half jaguar myself by now.

Everywhere I'd go, every park, passing by every vacant lot, taking a little walk in the jungle, I was automatically, almost unconsciously, looking at the shapes of blossoms, mushrooms, cacti, the Morning Glory trumpet-shaped look of the Datura in all of its varieties, its close cousins, Desfontainia (Intoxicator), iochroma, Methysticodendron (*Culebra Borrachero* – Serpent That Gets You Drunk), my hands reaching out and snapping off a blossom, carrying it to my mouth ... to the glee of my jaguar spirits. Now I can see what they wanted – my total and permanent transformation. But then I was still in a state of naïveté and innocence, acting automatically without seeing The Big Picture at all. It was as if my vision of the world was a box filled with jigsaw puzzle pieces that I very, very slowly was putting together into a coherent whole.

I stayed for a few days in Guayaquil and then took a bus up to Cuenca to meet Padre Crespi.

It was a long and arduous trip, a slow climb up from the coast into the Andes. I remember that the first lap lasted maybe five hours. Me and the Indians. No one else. No rest stops until we finally, after five hours, stopped at a restaurant and I went into the 'rest room' which was an open spot in a courtyard surrounded by high stone walls, and filled with pigs. You would have to do your stuff on the ground and then the pigs would come over and eat it. And, of course, pork was one of the main items on the menu in the restaurant next door. I did what I had to do and got back on the bus totally disgusted.

Not that Cuenca was much better.

It was way up in the Andes and I found a little *pensión*, got settled and, after one whole day's rest and recovery from the bus-ride, I went off in search of the *convento* where Crespi lived.

It was an old, colonial building and I couldn't believe what I saw, long lines of Indians standing waiting for handouts. Only what especially bothered me was what they were being handed – crackers, dry, saltine crackers. An Ecuadorian version of foodstamps. How could anyone survive on saltine crackers?

The Indian women themselves all wore beautifully woven skirts and 'mantas' (shawls), usually filled with rows of sun-symbols right out of the ancient Middle East/India:

Endless rows of the letter 'TI' – as in TI-A-NAKU.

But all the clothes were in rags now. The message was clear. The days of glory were over. We were now in the Age of the Conquerer, close to extinction. Were we on the threshold of some sort of Age of Indigenous Rebirth? Was that part of the larger picture that lay inside me in scattered jigsaw pieces?

I approached Crespi, surrounded by Indians. He must have been in his eighties, wearing a black cassock, bald, white-bearded. The Indians would touch his cassock and then kiss their fingers, as if he were some sort of miracle-working saint.

He finally noticed me and as I got closer to him I was assailed with the strong scent of urine. It wasn't fresh urine but old urine.

"I'm Hugh Fox/Hugo Fox," I said in Spanish, "from the US – *Los Estados Unidos*. I just read Von Däniken's *The Gold of the Gods* and I'd like to see some of the objects that the Indians have brought you from the caves."

"You're a professor of ... ?"

"Department of American Thought and Language, Michigan State University/*Departmento de Pensamiento y Lenguaje Americano, la Universidad de Michigan State*."

"Ahhhh," he answered, "welcome, welcome ..."

It was the perfect name. That's what it had been designed for – to impress. Also somewhat to conceal the fact that under the fancy title it was essentially a department of Freshman Comp, something that I barely understood until after I'd signed my contract. He handed one of the Indians his bag of crackers and took me by the arm into one of the buildings themselves, room after room filled with odd, eccentric-looking objects that – to be honest – from the very beginning I disbelieved in.

It wasn't merely the years of experience I had had studying ancient art, from about age 5 onwards, the Art Institute in Chicago, the museum at the Oriental Institute at the University of Chicago, museums in Mexico City, the Louvre, British Museum, all the years "in the field," so to speak, with Lucia, the walls of my old house in East Lansing filled with Mixtec, Zapotec, Chancay, Mochica pottery, but also the feelings that I shared with the jaguar-shaman art connoisseurs/cognoscenti inside me.

As Padre Crespi started to explain his objects my whole interior world was filled with negative snarls and growls, *no, this is all fraud, do not believe or trust this man, he has some sort of Messiah complex*, understanding without/beyond words.

But I listened anyhow, tried not to let the tremendous negative energies inside me spill out into the room.

"This is an Egyptian pharaonic boat," he went on, showing me a metal boat with metal figures in it that didn't look particularly Egyptian and certainly not pharaonic.

There were all sorts of wooden objects too, metal plates (copper?) with animals embossed on them, plates with Indus Valley/Andean Indigenous Script on them.

I remember turning one around and seeing *Hecho en Chile* stamped on it – Made in Chile. Chilean copper plate. Not particularly ancient ... certainly not pharaonic. An article already began to form in my head, an article that eventually came out in the *Western World Review*: "Von Däniken's Gold, Thar's Gold in Them Gods – An Objective Inquiry into the Possibility of Fraud and Trickery Regarding the Finding of Certain Pre-Columbian Artifacts and Caves in Ecuador," Vol.11, No.2, Summer 1977.

I was obviously face to face with major fraud. But I still didn't say anything, bided my time, let Crespi take me through his whole 'collection,' slowly coming to the conclusion that the man was totally senile. The urine smell was a good tipoff from the very beginning. But it was a very particular, peculiar sort of senility. Messianic pretensions, indeed! At the same time, there was an essential current of truth in the premise the whole 'collection' was based on – the fact that the Indus Valley Script was in use in the Andes, that there had been contact with, if not pharaonic Egypt, certainly pre-dynastic Egyptians. There were all sorts of Egyptian myths too about the Land of the Twin-Peaks in the West, the Land of the Setting Sun ... and there were the undeniable links between the Egyptian 'god' Osiris and his appearance in the New World under names like Quetzalcoatl (Mexico), Viracocha (Peru), Ra, Sua/Surya ... So there was a kernel of truth behind the fraud. My question was how did he pull it off, get even the minimal amount of knowledge that he needed to see/demonstrate any New World–Old World link in the first place?

I could have just left then and there but didn't, hung around, met a Dr. Landiver, a local M.D. with an extensive collection of *real* artifacts from the Indians in the Cuenca area. Landiver, in fact, told me "The Indians in this area didn't have any writing system in pre-Columbian times ... there are no caves ... Crespi is, you know ..." pointing to his head.

But it wasn't until my last day in Cuenca that I got a chance to get into Crespi's library and see whole shelves of materials on the Indus Valley civilisation, and I was told by one of the other priests there that Padre Crespi was originally from Italy, had studied archaeology before becoming a priest.

So there it was – the lost link.

I also noticed that the Indians in the Cuenca area were particularly gifted in metal-working and I concluded that what Crespi must have done was to 'invent' the artifacts of a whole fabricated culture and then have had local craftsmen actually manufacture them. It wasn't a small project but something that must have taken him years to bring to completion. Then enter Von Däniken just looking for a subject after his book on ancient astronauts. The two of them made a perfect pair, the archaeological fabricator meets the journalist fabricator, and the unsuspecting world out there, what are they to believe? What makes this sort of crime especially heinous is the fact that it contains any touch of truth at all.

I later noticed that Barry Fell, in his first edition of *America B.C.*, without ever having visited Ecuador the way I had and checking the whole story out, had swallowed the Crespi–Von Däniken fraud, hook line and sinker. In the latest edition of *America B.C.*, Fell has dropped the whole gold-of-the-gods in Cuenca story, but still retained one picture of an artifact from the Crespi 'collection.'

I was frustrated. I wanted more. It was an expensive trip for what I deemed no results.

I remember one afternoon walking out of town into the jungle which Crespi had pointed to when I'd asked him where the caves where the artifacts had been located actually were, leaving the town behind, moving further and further into the perpetual grey of the jungle itself, finding little footpaths/trails either human or animal, it was hard to say, trumpet-shaped flowers all around me, purple and yellow and red, all sorts of varieties and variations, again reaching out and starting to chew on a blossom here and there, swallowing, slowly beginning to change again, as if some sort of cellular conversion were taking place inside my soul, walking for hours, the sun going down and still walking, not sure if the light that I saw was moonlight or the night-sight light of my own augmented jaguar vision, beginning to see caves in my mind, below and around me, unsure whether I was in the jungle itself any longer or in the caves themselves, filled with a vision of vast caverns stretching out all around me, filled with beings like myself, only full-jaguars, like the black-belts of the jaguar-shaman world that I was still merely a neophyte in.

Was I really inside some sort of ancient Andean network that interconnected all the tribes and their psychic realities, or was it all a trick of the drugs?

I remember the sky beginning to change colour, from cadaverous white to a pale yellow (like some of the *borrachero* trumpet-blossoms themselves that I had eaten), and there in a dead clearing in front of me, one of those places in the jungle where nothing grows and some tribes have a deadly fear of, I saw a young woman walking toward me with bare breasts and beautifully muscular legs, long black hair, wide eyes ... Teresita ... finding myself running toward her as she ran toward me, at each step growing older and older, her sleek thighs wrinkling up, her breasts losing their fullness and hanging loose and empty, her black hair turning grey and then white. Not that I cared. I wanted her, at any age, at any moment, as long as I still was alive and able to want ... but at the moment when we would have met and fallen into each other's arms, she 'dissolved' and I fell down, cut my leg on a bamboo stake sticking up out of the ground, at first panicked, then sat there, ripped off the torn leg of my pants, watched it bleed and bleed until it clotted, slept for a while, the roars of the jaguarworld thundering inside me like the roar of some giant waterfall ... and then walked back to my *pensión*, packed and caught the bus back to Guayaquil.

It was a dramatic ride back. Going up into the Andes had been slow and torturous, but going back down was exhilaratingly terrifying, all stops out, full speed ahead, down long curves of mountain slopes and through endless banana groves as we got closer and closer to the coast, feeling confused and sick and disillusioned. I had followed the promptings of The Invisible World and what had it got me? What had I learned that I had to know?

In Guayaquil I went to the US Consul and asked her if she had ever heard anything about Crespi.

"Not much," she'd answered, a middle aged woman with short blonde-grey hair, wearing a tweed suit that seemed incongruously self-punishing in the Guayaquil coastal heat, "only that some years back he was caught sending out colonial paintings to the Vatican Museum, which was some sort of major crime. The 'national heritage' and all that. There was talk of prison but nothing came of it, his being a local 'holy man' and all ...but it seems to have deranged him. I wouldn't be at all surprised that the threat of prison was the source of his whole invention of Culture X ..."

"Well," I answered, my bandaged leg aching under a new pair of pants, part of my mind always focused on the wound, image-fighting against infection, imagining armies of my own phagocytes engulfing whatever invaders had entered into my body from outside, "Culture X exists ... or at least existed ... they used the same writing system in the Andes that they used in the Indus Valley Civilisation in what is today Pakistan ..."

"I know quite a bit about the Indus Civilisation," she interrupted me, "I've been to Mohejno Daro. Quite an interesting place. It seems to have been destroyed by outside invaders. Some people say the Aryans. But a connection to the Andes?"

"Two layers of connections," I answered back, quite aware that my credibility was vanishing quite rapidly in her eyes, "first the Dravidians/

Proto-IndoMediterraneans arrived here, and then the Aryans, the ultimate ancestors of the Incas. Tiawanaku was the sacred centre of all ancient myth ..."

She stopped, looked at me sceptically, then decided to be abruptly kind, got up, shook hands.

"Well, Professor, it's been fun. I'm sorry you were so disillusioned by your visit with Crespi. Ecuador has a way of disillusioning one. I must say that I don't have many illusions left myself," escorting me to the door, adding one last cynical "not even about ancient astronauts ... and navigators."

"Take care," I said, walking past her secretary-receptionist, out into the heavy, sodden heat of Guayaquil again.

Her reaction was typical of the reaction of almost everyone I would meet over the next decades – total disbelief. The idea that the New World had been populated exclusively by Siberians coming over the Bering Strait during the Ice Ages was as *ex cathedra* as the idea that the world was round or that the earth revolved around the sun and not vice versa. But there had been a time not long ago when it was just as dogmatic that the earth was the centre of the universe and that the sun and everything else revolved around *it!*

Perhaps I had a touch of my own personal messianism in me and wanted to emerge from all this (on a scholarly, not shamanistic level) as the Gaileo of Amerindian Pre-History, at last establishing what was the undeniable centricity of the Americas (with Tiawanaku as the centre of the centre) in ancient world religion – apart from whatever role I was or was not playing in what I suspected was to be a total change in the spiritual attitudes of the modern world, a change in the total direction of world spirituality.

I got on the plane the next day expecting an uneventful flight back to Los Angeles where I would transfer for a plane to Detroit, one short (twenty minute) last flight back to Lansing. There was one stop in Quito. The seat next to me was empty and in Quito a middle-aged man with a dark complexion and straight black hair (who could have been from either India or the Andes) got on and sat down next to me.

"So where are you coming from?" he asked me as we took off again.

"Cuenca," I answered, and told him the whole story about Von Däniken and Crespi, the whole business about the supposedly gold objects that had been brought from caves under the Andes and given to Crespi, as I was talking realising that, of course, the whole myth of bringing the objects to Crespi fitted perfectly into Crespi's role as local holy man (ancient, holy objects go to the reigning holy man, don't they?) concluding my remarks with "it just goes to show you how naïve I am! The caves are in my brain, not under the Andes!"

Which he thought was marvellously funny, laughing for a full five minutes, then sobering up, sitting back and telling me a story that was to become a major piece in the jigsaw puzzle of ancient lore that I was putting together in my mind. He made a very jovial, comforting companion after all I had been through, a beer in his hand, insisting on buying one for me. Which I was a bit worried about, afraid of mixing psychedelics with alcohol, but dismissing my fears and going along with his offer, the beer soothing and calming as I sat back and listened:

"Don't be too quick to dismiss stories about caves under the Andes. I am originally from La Paz myself and on Sundays my father would take me and my sister out into the countryside outside La Paz and a number of times we went into a cave at the foot of Mount Illimani. Inside there was a giant river. There must be a whole subterranean river-system under the Andes. And the river was so wide that we couldn't even throw a stone across it. Even my father couldn't throw a stone across it, this whole slowly moving mass of water and the high vaulted ceiling. It was pretty impressive. The natives have a myth about that particular cave. They say that every Spring a gold man with a bull's head emerges from the cave ..."

"Yama," I immediately answered, "the Hindu God of the Underworld. The same god who is pictured at Chavín."

"Well, I wouldn't be surprised if there were some sort of connection with Chavín. I'm an engineer and I don't know anything about Hindu myth, but as a matter of fact I wouldn't be surprised at *anything* when it comes to the geography of the Andes and the northern river basins, the Orinoco, Amazon, you know ..."

Indeed, I did know. Years before I was reading the Vishnu Purana, one of the ancient Hindu sacred books, and came across a section on the rivers of the Hindu Underworld and was especially struck by one passage that talked about the place where the white river meets the black river. Very specific. Very memorable. And then a few years afterward I had been lecturing on American Literature in Manaus and had taken a cruise on the Amazon and there was one place where you could see black water to your left and white water to your right, where the Rio Negro (which, flowing through the jungles, picked up all sorts of organic materials) met the Amazon. In Portuguese they called it *O Encontro Das Águas* – The Meeting of the Waters. And it perfectly fits the description of the meeting of the Black and White Rivers in Hindu sacred literature. If Tiawanaku was the Heaven of Hindu Myth, Mount Meru, could the Amazon Basin be its Hell? And were there actual river-connections between Tiawanaku/ Mount Illimani and, say, Chavín?

There was a young guy in front of us. Blond. The kind of bleach-job I used to see all the time when I taught at Loyola-Marymount – bleached from surfing. I actually had students who would surf all year around, come to an eight o'clock class in the middle of the winter after having been already out surfing for an hour or so.

He'd been listening to everything we had been talking about.

"Hey, man," he said, unbuckling his seat belt and getting up, turning around, kneeling on his seat, "let's get off in L.A. and take a plane right back. I've even got my scuba gear with me. Man, I'm willing to try anything ..."

"Well, I wish I could," I answered, "but I've got to get back. And I don't have unlimited funds ..."

"Neither do I," answered the engineer, "I'm on my way to Washington on business."

"Boy, what a bunch of deadheads!" said the surfer/scuba diver, "Just don't be surprised if you open up your morning paper some day and I'm in the headlines. 'Fools rush in where angels fear to tread' and all that ... and this is one fool who is hungry for fame."

Another young guy across the aisle from him turned around.

"Count me in!"

We could have formed an expedition right then and there. But didn't. And I've never opened up my newspaper, either morning *or* evening and seen anything about caves under the Andes, so I guess it was, as the Spanish saying goes, *mucho ruido, pocas nueces* – lots of noise, few nuts; a saying that is derived from the fact that the Spanish used to go around and shake nut-trees to bring down the ripe nuts and most of the time there was a lot of noise and few nuts.

The Bolivian and I talked a little bit about mutual friends we had in La Paz like Mariano Baptista, it started getting late, one of those all-night flights, and eventually they turned the lights off after a pretty decent meal, and I began to dream ...

I was wandering around in the jungle someplace, dark, dank, mysterious, when suddenly out of the underbrush jumped a man with his feet turned backwards, twisted so that his toes were where his heels were supposed to be. He had a big net in his hand and he threw if over me, the whole time grunting and laughing to himself, dragging me down to a river nearby, throwing me into a huge boat filled with hundreds of other 'victims' with their arms and legs bound, their mouths gagged, huddled silently back to back. I was pulled out of my net and tied and gagged and thrown in with the others as they cast off into a vast dark misty riverine world, lush with trees that overhung the water and blocked out whatever weak sunlight that was able to make its way in through the mists. It was a long journey down the river into a cave where we disembarked and our legs were unbound and we were all led inside a large temple without any windows so that the only light came from torches. We were all pushed and shoved down endless corridors inside the temple until we came to what seemed the temple's heart/centre where, under a huge monolithic stone carved in the shape of a jaguar, sat a man wearing a bull mask and carrying a trident in each hand. It was like being in Hell, and the man in the bull mask was the Devil, who then proceeded to separate us into various groups. The 'saved' and the 'damned'? I was obviously counted among the damned, screamed at in a language I didn't understand but which I suspected was Sanskrit, and then taken back into the underground riverworld, put on another boat and another voyage began to ...

I woke up.

Too much beer. My bladder was full. I got up and went back to the toilet, everyone on the flight asleep now. It looked like a giant hearse full of the dead. Hardly any lights on, the stewardesses asleep too. Was the plane on automatic pilot? Were the pilots asleep too?

I sat down on the toilet. Diarrhoea. Of course. I had a hyperactive bowel anyhow. I must have picked up some bug. There certainly were enough around.

But as I sat there I slowly realised (with the help of my inner-world jaguar mentors) that my dream hadn't been just dream but a kind of scholarly reconstruction.

The 'hunter' in the jungle with the net. Who was he? The Amazon was filled with stories about monsters with twisted feet, toes where the heels should be. Or if their feet weren't twisted front to back, they would have one leg, or one of their legs would be sharpened to a point. Among the Xingu the 'demon' with the sharpened, pointed leg was called Viti Viti and was associated with stone troughs that were always found along river banks, troughs that were very ancient and when I had seen them years before I had immediately associated with placer mining. The river water, bearing particles of gold from the Andes, would be shunted into these troughs where the gold would precipitate out. And where in ancient myth were there crippled gods? Among the Greeks, of course. Hephaistos, The Smith of the Gods, had his feet twisted so that the toes were where the heels should have been. The deformity was exactly the same in Greek and in some Amazonian myths. Smiths were ritually deformed. They were crippled in exchange for magic powers. Ancient smiths/metal workers were great magicians and their magic powers were associated with their deformities.

I remembered how the first name we have in history for Tiawanaku was *Anaku* – the Tin Lands.

So it wasn't just gold, was it, that was important for the ancients. But perhaps even more than gold, TIN!

I remembered one time when I was at Tiawanaku I had naively asked one of the Indians if there were any stories about dwarfs (*enanos*) associated with the ruins.

"Of course. They are called Ekkekos. They are hunchbacked and live in tunnels under the ruins. If you grab them they have to give you gold, because they are the Masters of Metals and they always possess great fortunes of gold. There were all sorts of openings into their tunnel-world under Tiawanaku. But they bothered the tourists so the tunnels were blocked (*tapados*) ... there is a whole dwarf cemetery over that way."

And he pointed over to a range of mountains in the distance.

I should have drawn a map, written down the directions, but I didn't.

What if there were some sort of ancient geo-political-economic 'structure' under all the ancient myths? The Devil/Yama is the Lord of the Underworld. Yama is "he who binds" in all ancient myths, associated with YAM, the sea. Like Tiawanaku/Meru he is on the other side of the ocean. What if ... if ... if ... Yama had been an actual king who was in charge of slave labour that was then supplied to the King of Tiawanaku, the Sun-King?

What if the ancient smiths were also the ancient slave-masters and the chief smith, Hephaistos in Greek, was also the chief slave-master who (as in Greek myth) actually worked for Helios, the Sun-King, the King of Tiawanaku?

Tiawanaku would have been Heaven, Chavín Hell and to be condemned to Hell was to be condemned to work until you died either in the mines or placer-mining gold.

The ancient myth-makers had listened to the stories that came back from the ancient reality of South America and transformed the reality into myth. What if all the stories about devils and gods and heavens and hells weren't derived from some sort of Jungian archetype, but from *the reality of ancient South America?*

Years before I had come across a Pueblo (Acoma) Indian myth in one of the Annual Reports of the US Bureau of Ethnology, Smithsonian

Institution ... a very strange piece about emerging from The Underworld through the place of emergence (the Shipap, the equivalent of the Hopi Sipapu) and finding themselves on the shores of a huge lake up in the mountains and in the distance was the City of the Gods ... of course, Tiawanaku ...

The myth went on to say that the Pueblo Indian gods (Katchinas) were actually attempts to replicate what the *real* gods at Tiawanaku had looked like in real life. It was an actual eye-witness account of Tiawanaku. But the important thing for me here was the fact that now the Pueblo Indian Underworld had become a geographical reality for me.

I finished what I had to do, took a little bottle of anti-diarrhoea pills that I always carried with me when I travelled, swallowed a couple of the pills, wiped myself and went back to my seat for the first time aware that, yes, there had been a *why* to this whole trip. I had been told that there were caves under the Andes. Was that where the Immortals were living now?

When I got back to East Lansing, I expected a fortune to be waiting for me.

Harper's Magazine Press had not only bought *The Gods of the Cataclysm* (and given me a princely advance) but had accepted a second volume. The first volume Larry Freudlich had labelled *The Gods of the Cataclysm* (to pick up some readers from the audience that read books like Von Däniken's *The Chariots of the Gods* and *The Gold of the Gods*) and had originally been called *Indians: The Pre-Historic Links*. The second had been called *Indians: The Migratory Record*, all about obvious traces that the migrating peoples out of Asia had left behind in the South Seas, the endless ruined temples, pyramids that were close cousins to the temples and pyramids of South and Middle America. And I was just waiting for Freudlich to come up with another title with "gods" in it – *The Myths of the Gods*, something like that. I even had a third volume half written about the astrological star-map significance of ancient epics, the whole business about the key to ancient myth being the passage of the sun through the zodiac to the solstice-point House of the Sun, Tiawanaku.

Only when I got back, instead of good news waiting for me, there was a letter from Brockman about Harper's Magazine Press going bankrupt and wanting the third of the advance back that they had given me for the second book.

That's the way you always get advances from publishers, the first bundle when they take the book, the second when you hand in the finished manuscript, the third when the book finally comes out.

It may have been fair. After all they weren't going to publish the book. But I had already spent the money on new carpeting for our old house – new carpeting, a new roof, a new furnace.

So I wrote to Brockman, he talked to Freudlich and rather than waste more money trying to get blood out of a turnip (me), they just let it go. It was a big disaster scenario for them anyhow; a little more disaster hardly mattered.

The book on myths eventually was transformed into a book I called *Voyage to the House of the Sun* but which the publisher (Edwin Mellen Press) changed into *The Mythological Origins of the Epic Genre: The Solar Voyage as the Hero's Journey*. Studies in Epic and Romance Literature, Vol.1, Lewiston, New York, 1989.

But Mellen paid in copies not cash.

It was almost like a conspiracy. The American consciousness that I was watching change like an emerging butterfly right before my eyes was now reverting back to an earlier pupa phase. The total revolution of consciousness wasn't happening.

No one seemed to care that Columbus had been somewhat right in calling Indians Indians, that the same voyage that he had made had been made by endless raft and/or boat-loads of people out of India and the Mediterranean in very ancient times.

Reading Lahovary's *Dravidian Origins and the West* I had come across the fact that ancient India and the Mediterranean and parts of Black Africa had been inhabited by more or less the same people, what he and H. Heras (in *Studies in Proto-Indo-Mediterranean Culture*, Bombay: Indian Historical Research Institute, 1953) had called Proto-Indo-Mediterranean man. Call them the Mother Goddess People.

Proto-Indo-Mediterranean man had formed the sub-strata of the major cultures in South America ... and reading L.A. Waddell's *The Makers of Civilization in Race and History* (Delhi: S. Chand & Co., 1968) I'd even come across the absolutely weird, mindboggling fact that the first pre-dynastic Sumerian king had been named Ra and Kon, the same name that was associated with the sun-king Viracocha-Quetzalcoatl in the New World, Egypt and the South Seas.

The picture of one of the immortals began to form in my mind.

Ancient Peru-Bolivia had been filled with statues of this god-man when the Spaniards had first arrived and the sixteenth century Spaniards had compared him to St. Bartholomew – tall, bearded, white, wearing a kind of 'tunic' and sandals. I had searched the records for a portrait of St. Bartholomew, had never found one ... and the Spaniards themselves had destroyed all the statues of Viracocha-Ra-Con that they had found, afraid that this 'god-man' would serve as a rallying-point around which anti-Spanish resistance might form during the Conquest.

But still, I had a vague notion of what one of the immortals had looked like. He was Helios, the sun-god in Greek myth, wasn't he? Osiris in Egyptian myth! Or Ra himself? There was yet another portrait that *had* survived, the Old Fire God:

Perhaps he was the 'god' who has come down to us mythically as Hephaistos? Or was this perhaps a portrait of Ra-Viracocha himself? True, the Spaniards had destroyed all the portraits of Ra-Viracocha that were available to them, but many of the portraits of this old bearded "fire-god" (which may have been another way of saying "sun-god!") had been buried and not unearthed until post-colonial times. Later I would unearth his true identity myself, but even back then in the late seventies, I began to have a sense of reaching out through the ages, almost able to touch (see) one of the original "gods" – Votan-Ra-Viracocha (or Hephaistos) himself. And wasn't I beginning to see, in the crowds of jaguars that circled through my consciousness, an old man with tiger-jaguar fangs off in the shadows, backstage as it were, slowly, ever so slowly beginning to make his way on to the stage, looking at me with burning penetrating jaguar eyes? So here I was with the most important secrets ever to be unearthed in my hands, and nobody else was interested. The past, unless it was framed in terms of ancient astronauts, didn't seem to interest anyone. It was almost like some sort of demonic conspiracy against consciousness-raising had invaded the modern world.

Everything was hardware, weaponry, electronics, and I and some of my poet-shaman friends seemed to be the only ones who realised that the secrets of survival lay not in anything "Out There," but in changes that could be effected (as the ancients had done it) on a somatic, cellular, atomic level. The work of Cleveland mystic D.A. Levy was filled with images that could have come out of my own psychedelic consciousness:

> The mist of the sacred lake is hidden in the mind
> the stream of the sacred lake is like the hot breath
> of a backed-up sewer when seen by the lion unconscious of his form
>
> Hail, – the lion with second sight, the lion who
> stands in the doorway of tomorrow, the lion of precognition
> who sees nothing ...
>
> Hail, – the lion of the mirror room
> the lion of the mat-ear
> & the lion who watches from his lair on the rim of the eon-sea ...

("The Litany of the Green Lion," in *The Living Underground: An Anthology of Contemporary American Poetry*, ed. by Hugh Fox. Troy, New York: Whiston Publishing Co., 1973, p.256.)

> when leaving the body
> one goes to the
> Lotus of a Thousand Petals
> getting there one must cross
> his own mountains

everyone gets there
EVENTUALLY
one leaves the body

one may leave the body by leaving the body
he writes 'EXIT' on his toe
he writes 'EXIT' on his navel
i leave by the crown of thorns
(this is the aperture of Brahma)
this is the Brahmarandhra
this is the way of the Tibetan monk
leaving the body ...

THE LIGHT moves
like the wind
moves clouds suns moon mountains water
moves like birds to an internal island
that is found with the eye
one can reach the island by going there
(this is the time of the great light)

("The North American Book of the Dead, Part I", also in the *Living Underground* anthology, pp.233-235.)

I had visited Levy in Cleveland in the summer of 1968 on the way to East Lansing and then Providence/Brown University. Of course I had begun to see everything symbolically. I was leaving the City of Angels to go to Providence ... *providere* ... to see before ... 'to be guided' ...

His entire apartment was one huge psychedelic trip. There wasn't one square inch that wasn't painted in wild, swirling colours.

Levy himself was thin, ascetic, as pale as a cloud. We hardly talked. We didn't have to. We 'communed' with each other across wide spectrums of ultra-conscious communication.

And then, in the Fall of 1968, Levy put a gun in his mouth (like Hemingway had done) and pulled the trigger. The anti-consciousness-raising conspiracy was taking over again, the pragmatic-scientific demons were taking the reins of power in their hands again. The total society revolution that I had believed was taking place was slowly not only being stopped, but reversed. I still tried to maintain a positive, optimistic outlook, but in an essay I wrote called "US Iconography and the Yippie

Media Termites" that appeared in a special issue of *TriQuarterly (Literature in Revolution)* in Winter/Spring 1972, I obviously was well aware that the reaction of the Post-Modern Empirical Beast Consciousness that dominated the day-to-day running of the US was violently reacting to the New Expanded Consciousness (that had unfortunately become increasingly identified with the New Left) that had tried to invade and replace it:

> The danger of the New Left is not in its present violence, but in its awakening in the Beast a moral sense ... when this disease of politicisation first began to spread and the Beast became increasingly aware of its own beastliness, it first hated itself, then the hate turned to self-acceptance. Now acceptance has become defiance and the Beast's whole organic structure is relegated to one function – the survival and triumph of bestiality ... at any cost ...
> (p.429)

The reality that most people saw most of the time was obviously false, partial, incomplete. The world was obviously really made out of agates and amethysts. 'Souls,' 'spirits,' 'presences' weren't merely the dead wood of ancient religions updated, but part of the flux and flow of Time Present that swirled and vortexed around us. I even asked myself what was really behind the Resurrection of Jesus, the descent into Hell and then the re-ascent into "Heaven" ... and the promise that if you "believe," the Holy Spirit will enter into you and you will receive ETERNAL LIFE.

The whole idea of communion, eating God's body and drinking his blood, seemed to have ancient, pre-Christian roots. The Aztec word for the psychedelic mushroom that transported them into an ecstatic seventh heaven, after all, was Teonanacatl, the Flesh of the Gods.

I began to live in a totally schizoid state. I was simultaneously in East Lansing, Michigan and in Tiawanaku–the Caves Under the Andes. I was moving toward the end of the seventies on what I might call an Unreal-Time Time-Track, but my essential inner core existed in a timeless state of communion with the visionings of the ancients.

In a sense I had believed and the Holy Spirit had entered into me and totally transformed my life.

The Datura seeds I had scattered in my backyard had grown and produced their own seeds, and every Fall I began to harvest them so that I seldom really 'descended' into what most people would have called 'Real-Time' at all. On the surface I was a stable, 'normal' university professor teaching what had become a course in The Pre-Columbian Past, getting my students to research and write about the materials that I was, in a sense, living full time inside of, the father of two little girls, with a beautiful new wife ... while on another, subterranean level I was living practically full time inside The Vision of Immortality that I shared with what might be called The Jaguar Shaman-Nation inside me.

My wife, Nona, very well understood what was going on because I had taken her inside my secrets and she had started to inhabit the jaguar vision-world with me.

I have written extensively about my personal life elsewhere in a book called *The Confessions* which (perhaps fortunately for my career) has remained for the most part unpublished. The manuscript is in Special Collections in the library at Michigan State, and some idea of the full complexity of the reality I was living made its way into poems I wrote under yet another alternate identity, Connie Fox*, an androgynous identity that I discovered was an integral part of shamanistic psychology, so there is no point in expanding on that part of my 'schizoidness' here, but suffice it to say that Reality had developed into multiple layers and facets for me. I could handle it. I seemed to have been made precisely to handle it. My wife, however, entered precariously into this world at her own risk – with serious negative consequences for her entire future.

She was (and is) a brilliant woman, finished her Ph.D. in American Literature a few years after she married me – two little girls and all. Beautiful woman. All textures and seduction, black tights and black suede, stretch lace, mesh, wildly orgasmic, fetishistic, very tactile, loving, almost engulfing with the two girls.

And as brilliant as she was she understood very well just how urgent my need was to return to South America.

I remember her one night, after the girls had been put to bed, stretching out on the big bed in my room, like a black panther in her black velour top and robe and black lycra tights, speculating on my speculations:

"So it might mean that what we call Christianity with its structure of Heaven and Hell, saviour and angels on one side and Satan and his demons on the other, is actually a hand-me-down – through Judaism – of the *reality* of ancient South America. I know personally, since I have

---

*   *Blood Cocoon* (Zahir, 1980), *The Dream of the Black Topaze Chamber* (Abraxas, 1981), *Oma* (Implosion Press, 1985), *10 to the 170th* (Trout Creek Press, 1986), *Babicka* (Kangaroo Court Press, 1986), *Nachthymnen* (Mudborn Press, 1986), *Our Lady of Laussel* (Spectacular Diseases Press, England, 1991), *Entre Nous* (Trout Creek Press, 1992).

stepped into 'psychedelia,' I feel almost as surrounded by 'presences' as you say you do. And they aren't all benevolent. I keep thinking of Grimm's *Germanic Mythology*, the Götterdämmerung, Wagner ... like the last scene in Götterdämmerung, the Rhine overflowing its banks ... I keep thinking of the way Posransky found Tiawanaku, everything covered with mud as if 'other' gods, the water-, not the sky-gods, had destroyed the Sun-Kingdom ... I think we should go back to the Andes at any cost and get into the cave system itself and face whatever is left there ... our notions of Heaven and Hell remain so vague, always 'Out There' somewhere ... what if ... if ... they are real places in Real Time ... even if the 'gods' were destroyed, the caves under the Andes are the last great frontier in world archaeology. We know they are there, from all the Hopi legends, we know that they were inhabited, we know that Anaku was the tin lands ... Posnansky speculates that the walls of the buildings at Tiawanaku were covered with gold plates ... there are all the legends about dwarf miners ... who can say what treasures still exist in the caveworld under the Andes ..."

Nona was becoming as much a scholar of the ancient world as I was. She should have begun to write articles and books about American literature. The job situation was precarious and highly competitive. Instead she began to immerse herself in ancient literature in both the New and Old Worlds, study the tribes that were the most isolated from the modern world and which we both saw as the linear descendents of the ancient Holy People – tribes like the Kogi and Desaná.

We both began to apply for grants. She applied for a Fulbright to South America but ended up getting a teaching job for a year in Valencia, Spain. Of course I went along, lectured throughout Spain on contemporary American literature – which in reality was merely talking about my poet friends in the "movement."

We went to Tunisia, Tunis, visited the site of ancient Carthage, went to Cadíz, the ancient Phoenician city of Gadés ... the whole Carthaginian/ Punic thrust out into the Atlantic took on a new dimension of reality for me, laid the foundations for one of my most unexpected and dramatic later discoveries, the fact that Mochica Indian pottery on the northern Peruvian coast was filled with scenes from Herakles myths – and Phoenician writing. More about that later.

There were whole years that I saw merely as 'interludes,' years of scholarly preparation for the revelations I was about to make. I began to study Hebrew, Sumerian, Arabic. The years passed like days, the little girls became young women.

In 1978 I got a grant to teach at the Universidade Federal de Santa Catarina in Florianópolis, Brazil.

I was teaching at the university and Nona got a job teaching at a local language school – The Fiske Academy.

It was a strange place, the island of Santa Catarina. Just off the southern Brazilian coast, but close enough to the mainland for them to build a connecting bridge.

Was there any 'pattern' in my life, I began to wonder, or was it all just chaos, chance, confusion? Had I been 'brought' here? Was there a reason I had spent a year in Spain/North Africa? What was I doing now in this tropical paradise, an island rimmed by beaches, all palms and high rises (and the inevitable slums)?

I began to feel pulled toward the coves on the Atlantic side of the island, as if there were hidden *whys* behind everything that had happened to me in the last few years. I had brought large supplies of Datura seeds with me but began to discover that the island itself was nicely stocked with other psychedelics. I seldom 'came down.' The island became a kind of paradise for me. My jaguars were in their own seventh heaven.

My colleagues, Dilvo Ristoff, Hilario Bohn, Bernadette Passold, would be amused by me, the Outsider, "L'Etranger," having come to *their* island, going on a picnic, walking off by myself and coming back with the little notebook I carried everywhere with me, filled with drawings of petroglyphs that I would inevitably find everywhere around me, the lost hieroglyphs of The Ancients that sometimes I felt had been left there specifically for me, as if everything that was happening was part of some larger divine design.

I remember showing Hilario one drawing I'd found during a picnic outing on the island of Campeche:

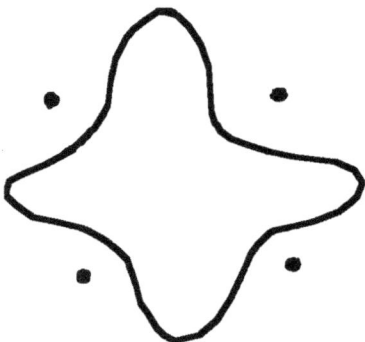

"What's that, something drawn on the rocks by missionaries? It's kind of lopsided, isn't it?" Hilario laughed, taking my notebook and thumbing through it. "And what's all this about?"

Circle variations:

"They are all variations of the same theme," I explained. "The top one is a Venus symbol, the circles are sun symbols/letters …"

"Letters?" he asked cynically. "This is all pre-Columbian stuff, right?"

"They're various Middle Eastern-Indus Valley Civilisation ways of writing TI. Sometimes it's a circle with a dot in the middle, sometimes a circle with an X, sometimes a circle with a cross. All part of the same 'message' – the year, life itself, centres around the 'death' and 'rebirth' of the sun. And there is this subtle but essential connection to Venus, Hun Hunapu among the Maya. At the time of the Winter Solstice, when the sun symbolically 'dies,' Venus disappears, and then the days begin to get longer, the sun is 'reborn,' so the ancients assumed that Venus had *become* the new sun …"

"Very interesting," said Hilario, "you seem to have an inordinate interest in the Pre-Columbian, you *and* your charming wife!"

I remember Nona smiling, a beer in one hand, a beef rib in the other. "The way I see it, what we consider today as somewhat vague and airy 'theology' is all derived from a very real, concrete ancient reality. What actually went on at Tiawanaku, Bolivia and in the caves under the Andes that connected to the Amazon and other river valley and the Peruvian coast (and Chavín) in ancient times was transformed into all subsequent myths and theologies …"

"Tiawanaku?" smiled Hilario, not a malicious man but amused by anything dead serious and solemn. "I've never been there … it's not very easy to get there from La Paz …"

Married to a Bolivian from Cochabama, and he'd never been to Tiawanaku. If nothing else came from all my discoveries, I felt at that moment, if all the rest *was* undirected chaos, at least my discoveries, if they were ever accepted, would restore Tiawanaku to its rightful place in world myth. But Hilario was typical. New York wasn't interested, the university quarterlies weren't interested. If I'd been writing articles about Rilke or Marguerite Duras my work would have been published everywhere, only as it was what I *was* writing didn't fit into any preconceived slot and consequently no-one wanted it. It really was quite true that if a new book came out on Napoleon, it was time to write the next one – the market niche had been created.

We rented a house in the middle of the jungle on the island, with a verandah on the back that looked out on forests of pines and eucalyptus. I was happy in my own minor way. It was romantic for Nona and me and the girls. And then one day Nona brought home the woman who was to replace her and who, to this day, I believe is Doña Teresita (Teresinha in Portuguese) in another transmuted, somehow 'reincarnated' form …

"Maria Bernadette has just finished my course at Fiske," said Nona, "and I was wondering if you'd be willing to do a little tutoring with her."

Of course this was before I knew who was really 'hidden' inside Maria Bernadette's (nicknamed "Dette") skin. She was dressed all in white, tiny, very clinical looking. It was a perfect disguise. How could I have ever guessed that inside this rather boring, diminutive shell was concealed the Power and the Glory of the Immortals?

"I'm so overworked already," I said.

And I was. Finding the 'markers' of the Winter Solstice people everywhere along the Santa Catarina coast, beginning to see the Amazon as the River Thermadon in Greek myth, the river that led to the Land of the Sun-King, beginning to find links between Amazonian tribes and Indonesia and the rest of the Orient.

Was it by accident that the proto-Amerindian word for fire, K(w)ati/a, matched up with the Japanese K'waji? I think not.* I think B.J. Meggers, Clifford Evans Jr. and Emilio Estrada were 100% on track comparing prehistoric Japanese (Jomon) pottery with the pottery on the Ecuadorian coast (in their *Early Formative Period of Coastal Ecuador*, 1965). Now I was on the track of tracing the proto-Japanese into the Amazon, feeling very rushed, trying to teach classes in American Literature that I really couldn't have cared less about. What I mainly did, in fact, was to teach the very contemporary, which meant my fellow Hippy Visionaries – Lifshin, Levy, John Bennett, Smith, Morris, A. D. Winans, Joseph Bruchac (who also just happened to be an American Indian). I even was in the process of founding a journal called *Ilha do Desterro – Exile's Island* that dealt

---

* See Esther Matteson, et al, *Comparative Studies in Amerindian Languages*, The Hague-Paris: Mouton, 1992.

exclusively with the post-Beat writers I called the Invisible Generation, a journal that, as a matter of fact, still is in existence, although, sadly enough, the last issue I saw didn't even mention me as the Founding Father.

So with my time and energy divided between the Pre-Columbian and the very contemporary, I was feeling very rushed and pushed, really didn't want any more intrusions into my little world.

But Nona insisted.

"Come on, be a sport."

I felt embarrassed. That was one of her techniques that usually worked. And it certainly worked this time. I gave in.

"OK ... we can start next week .."

"Why don't you come next week to my place. I can make coffee ..."

Her voice sounded more like a tangled purr than a voice and when she touched my hand as she said goodbye she dug her nails ever so slightly into my palm.

She was an M.D., specialising in reconstructive surgery and when I began to see some of the patients she had worked on, I was utterly amazed at her abilities to reconstruct/restore. Like, I remember, a few months later walking down the street with her and a woman coming up to her and kissing her, throwing her arms around her, "Doctor Bernadette, it's so wonderful to see you ..."

"You too," she said, looking carefully at the woman's face, "it's coming along very nicely ..."

"It's a miracle," the woman had said, kissing Bernadette again, "I thank you so much ..."

After the woman had left I asked her what that was all about.

"She had a terrible cancer on her face and I did a radical surgery, cut the whole thing out and pulled the remaining tissue over to cover it up. It looked all twisted and terrible for about a year, but gradually the tissue stretched, and now ..."

"I couldn't see anything," I had to admit, "she looked perfectly normal to me."

Which was the kind of a role you would have expected Teresinha to have assumed into another reincarnation/avatar/form – the role of restorer ... saviour.

When we did go over to her place the following week to begin a course in conversational English, I couldn't believe the change. It was as if she had read my mind and clothed herself to fulfil all my most subterranean desires. She was all in black, some kind of Japanese or Chinese silk wedgie shoes, black lycra legs, a black silk dress, her thick tigerish hair brushed out, not heavily made up, but all the lines and shadows in the right places, feline, jaguarish, pantherish.

She and Nona (on purpose or by chance?) looked very much alike, and Bernadette's whole apartment seemed little more than an extension of her feline nature. Everything oriental, Japanese, Chinese. The perfect complement to exactly match the influences on the New World that I was studying. It all fitted together like a perfectly carved piece of Chinese wood work.

Her English was good and she said that she was planning to go to Canada with her brother, Luis, who was going to get a Ph.D. in Electrical Engineering at the University of Waterloo, but in the next months, as we got to know each other better and better, her plans slowly changed.

And I should explain that Nona also began to change, discover new avenues and vistas within her psyche.

Within six months, Bernadette (Dette) had moved in with us and the main bedroom of our house in the middle of the jungle had become the centre of psychosexual innovation and experimentation.

The both of them encouraged my feminine side. I was too restricted and monopolar for them. I was re-baptised as Connie and more and more began to move into new psychosexual roles and dimensions.

It's a time I've written about (as Connie Fox) in a novel called *The Dream of the Black Topaze Chamber* (unpublished) and a book of poetry published by Ghost Pony Press in 1983, with me as Connie on the cover.

The poetry itself tells it all, how, somehow, our space on the Island of Santa Catarina at the end of the 1970s was transformed into the City of the Gods. The imagery is there and says it all:

> Eyes open on
> beryl
> (lined-room)
> emerald-green, pale green,
> passing to light-blue, yellow,
> white, pale rose pink ...
> I'm moving up from
> a lake shore toward a
> city of (byzantium?) gold ...
> (p.6)

The city of gold, of course, is Tiawanaku. What had happened was that Tiawanaku had, in a sense, been reborn in us, and slowly, in the chill winter Santa Catarina nights with the heater on in our huge room, on the huge black silk sheeted bed, under the influence of the sacred plants that surrounded us in the jungle, whispering out to us to be used, we all assumed new forms, and I realised that the Doña Teresa that I had seen so many years before in the Peruvian Montaña was merely one form of an eternal spirit (person) that transcended space and time.

That was the secret of the gods, the whole idea behind the multiple 'avatars' or forms that seemed at first so bewildering in classical Hinduism. There wasn't just one Siva or Vishnu, but the essential Siva-Vishnu spirit that then assumed different forms.

It was the same idea of taking the sacred drug and assuming a jaguar form (jaguar-shaman) but extended out beyond the jaguar into other human identities so that the same essential 'spirit' could, in a sense, secrete different 'bodies' around it without changing its core identity.

Life for all of us became Zen fulfillment:

into
black topaze
transformation ...
brotando out of the atavistic
flesh-soil of
Dravidian All-Gods,
focused only in this
moment of latticed beryl
black and green.
(p.9)

Brotando is Portuguese for "sprouting." Sometimes I'd think in Portuguese, sometimes in English. The transition from Spanish to Portuguese was effortless, "falar" instead of "hablar," "os moments" instead of "los momentos," minor changes in pronunciation instead of major changes in vocabulary and syntax.

What we had essentially done was allow the sacred drugs to transport us into immortality NOW. We had escaped the falseness of The Modern and returned to a moment-by-moment interfacing with the divinity that for most of mankind most of the time was concealed (and never seen) in the very essence of the world around us.

Everything became divinised, the forest around us, the serpents, birds, our own flesh. I perfectly understood at last what the receiving of the Holy Spirit within me (us) really meant, the end of all dualistic tuggings between flesh and spirit, in fact a kind of divinisation of the flesh itself:

> ... Angor-Wat Garudian green-wings
> rustling up the floresta [forest]
> rising with a huge
> rush, sigh
> water in the Great Goddess
> moonfields of Orangutan lushness.
> I believe in wolf-spiders in
> banana groves and the turning of
> papaya into perfumed gold
> full of the wedge-arrows of
> bird-bites, the agates of
> eggplants and the teeth of
> corn, the goddesses of the
> rain-garden baring their
> breasts and receiving us in
> the glistening beaded caves
> of their wombs ...
> I believe that it all comes, that it
> was made to come, that my glands secrete
> the gods and my closed-eyed inner ecstasy
> is the why of creation.
> (p.14)

It's easy to see now, looking back, that I should have accepted the job offer that I had received from the University of Santa Catarina. Santa Catarina *could* and *had* become for us our own private Home of the Gods. We had moved back through Capitalism and Scientism, Empiricism, through the Age of Faith, the Age(s) of Philosophy, beyond the world of the Father God(s), to the Mother Goddess World of pure instantaneous existentialism.

Look at the very last lines in section 26 of *The Dream of the Black Topaze Chamber*:

> ... we preserve ourselves
> inviolate ... inside the core or orgasming crystal
> at one with our realness,
> at odds
> forever with the

hierophantic scales of their
unrealness.
(p.15)

Only then, we made the fatal mistake of trying to transport our private, interiorised Home of the Gods, our Black Topaze Chamber, back into the heart of the Beast again. We returned to East Lansing.

Dette and Nona had both studied gem-cutting with a master gem-cutter in Florianópolis, and once back in Michigan they opened a store and tried to sell (and cut) gems, started a dress business that might have succeeded if they had known anything about business. Nona was supposed to have her job waiting for her in the Department of American Thought and Language, but, of course, it wasn't. And Dette, once she had got a good look at the exaggerated bureaucratic-capitalistic structure of American hospitals, had decided to forget Medicine altogether and design dresses.

We had been 'gods' living in the midst of a divine jungle, and now suddenly we had taken on 'mortality' again and stepped right back into the middle of industrial America, a couple of miles down the road from the Oldsmobile plant, surrounded by all the electronic capitalistic clutter and clatter of the end of the twentieth century.

The shift was too abrupt, the demands too exaggerated.

Nona began to crack. In the Black Topaze Chamber we were all the same sex, the same timeless divine sexual plasm living in the midst of the aura of the Great Goddess, Mother Earth, Mother Sea. We were like the Kogi Indian wisemen (The Mamas) who, from the time they are born, never see the light of the day and are continually kept under the influence of Coca, living in a state of unbroken visionary ecstasy. And now suddenly we were withdrawn from all the divinity that surrounded us and thrust into the kleig-light brightness of decadent, exaggerated mechanisation and industrialisation.

Dette-Teresinha somehow preserved her millennial inviolateness in spite of her being thrust so violently into the blinding light of The Modern (Post-Modern), but Nona 'cracked,' began to hang on Dette-Teresinha, wanted to form some sort of nest-world with just her, isolate herself from me.

I tried to comfort her, rebond with her.

I had been trying to get Dette-Teresinha pregnant.

Both women wanted Dette-Teresinha to have a child and, in fact, that moment of attempted impregnation was always the ritual high-point of all our trinitarian lovemaking.

I wrote a novel called *Trinity* (still unpublished) all about the three of us as a kind of trinity, three separate persons in one godhead – and sometimes I thought that Dette-Teresinha's having a child was part of some invisible purpose of the immortals for having brought us all together in the first place. Perhaps what I had begun to think of as my messianic role of revealing the truth about the ancient Tiawanakan past was to be fulfilled by He Who Was Yet to Come. Now I began to wonder if Judeo-Christian messiah-theology was somehow connected to the 're-birth' of a messiah who would transform the whole world into the New Earth and New Covenant that was in everyone's deepest, secret dreams. Perhaps what was about to happen wasn't merely the revelation of the existence or whereabouts of The Immortals, but the transformation of the whole planetary consciousness, the final elevation of Mankind to the fulfilment of its latent potentialities.

But Dette-Teresinha never got pregnant and one night, trying to comfort Nona, who had moved into a state of grey depression most of the time, on a sudden impulse we had sex and *she* became pregnant.

I called the boy Christopher, and although for years I had not been a practicing Catholic, I started going back to church and had the boy baptised at the local parish in East Lansing. Christopher, of course, means "Christ-Bearer" and I thought there was a strong possibility that he would be the agent of universal transformation as Mankind moved over the edge of the Third Millennium.

Everywhere I looked I saw the sacred turned into the profane. Coca (Cocaine) had become Crack-Cocaine and the whole modern world was slowly evolving into a state of anarchy. The prison population in the US had reached extravagant proportions and the cities of God had become the cities of Madness. The early American dream of finding a New Jerusalem in the New World had been turned into a violent, bloody nightmare. The city of Nuestra Señora de los Ángeles (Our Lady of the Angels), Los Angeles, had become a sad centre of gang violence ... and everywhere it was the same. The holy names were there, Saint Francis (San Francisco), St. Louis, Providence, Salem (Jerusalem), Saint Anthony (San Antonio) ... and even in the names that weren't involved directly with saints and holiness, there was always a sense of newness, freshness, starting things all over again – NEW York, NEW Mexico, NEW Hampshire ... only the dream had been perverted and twisted and the only thing new that had emerged from the contemporary Americas was new levels of violence and depravation.

Israel was in a state of either outright or muted war with her neighbours, much of Africa was in a state of anarchy, the millennial conflicts in the

Balkans had become bloody yet again ... and here I was, in the midst of all this madness, understanding what chemicals were needed to really enable mankind to reach Teilhard de Chardin's "Omega Point." Over and over again in my poetry, as in this poem "Vision," I would touch on the idea of universal chemical revolution/rebirth:

> I call the directives of the eucalyptus and the fig
> from the messianic hills suspended between
> mountain and sea,
> this is the afternoon of ascension, the night of
> epiphanal winged unfolding, to shape the word
> NOW is the ultimate crucifixion, to breathe in and
> out the clarity of the rising moon, to sink into the
> patchwork-vined arroyos still vertiginously green in
> the midst of drought... I abolish geography and
> recentre us in the omphalos of solstice spinning
> Taipe-Cola space, the stone at the centre of our lives
> here in the arroyos of the cold sun laced between gulls
> and hawks, the dispersion ends and in our aging we return
> to fur and whispers, mandala within mandala, spider silk
> gleams in the morning wind, breakfast becomes the breaking
> of the bread of our barrierless selves, as Time iridesces
> out into sacks of thinnest infinity.

(Collected in *The Sacred Cave and Other Poems*, Omega Cat Press, Cupertino, California, 1992, p.14)

One time when I had been to Tiawanaku I had asked one of the Aymara Indians (whose language is a variant of Turkish, which demonstrates yet again the link between Anatolia/Asia Minor/Turkey and the Andes) what Tiawanaku meant for him and he had answered "For us the name isn't Tiawanaku but Taipe Cola, the Stone in the Middle," and I had even found this same idea of centricity in the name Tiawanaku itself ... in Caribbean (Trinidadian, etc.) words for centre, like *Nak*. (See L. Douay's *Nouvelles Recherches Philologiques Sur L'Antiguite Americaine*, Paris: J. Maison Neuve, 1900)

Looking back at this poem I find it interesting that I talk about "abolishing geography," with the implication that somehow the idea, the "spirit" of Tiawanaku was to become universalised, not confined to a place on the Tropic of Capricorn, but spread across the entire globe.

At any rate, the boy was born and peace descended on our home for a time until strange changes began to take place in Nona herself and what she tried to do was break the trinitarian nature of our pact and somehow bond solely with Teresina-Bernadette – which, of course, could not be.

We had actually made a three-way vow in Brazil before we had come back to the US. I remember it very well, the three candles on a table on the verandah on the back of our house in the jungle, bats flying through and above the trees that surrounded us, under a full moon, the three of us joining hands and repeating the liturgy we had earlier written down –

ONE FOR ALL AND ALL FOR ONE,
ALWAYS AND ALWAYS UNTIL LIFE IS DONE,
REBORN, TRANSFORMED IN WHATEVER WAYS,
UNIFIED OUR LIVES, OUR THOUGHTS, OUR DAYS …

Now old, hidden needs began to surface in Nona. Old, hidden 'dependencies.' She needed a woman, she said, and she needed a woman all to herself. Somehow, in the way she had been raised, her psychological needs had always remained truncated. Perhaps a three-way, trinitarian relationship was too much to expect from anyone, but at any rate whatever she needed was not being fulfilled in the trinity of our lives as we were living them in East Lansing in the middle of the 80s, and so she went out and found another woman and declared herself to be a lesbian, left the house, broke, and for a while became our declared enemy.

To describe what happened next would require a whole book in itself, and, as a matter of fact I have written a number of novelistic treatments of the events, all of them unpublished: *And the Lord Said Unto Satan*, *Voyage to the House of Yama* and *The Thirteen Keys to Talmud*.

I slowly began to see the woman who Nona had paired up with as 'demonic,' and the whole breakup of our trinitarian relationship as a manifestation of negative, counter-forces in the invisible world that surrounded us. The war between Good and Evil wasn't over. If the 'gods' still lived either in some one place in or under the Andes or (as in the case of Teresinha) in transmuted, transformed forms, so did the 'demons.'

The eternal war between the Life- and Death-Forces, between the Gods and Anti-Gods continued and I felt I was caught in the very midst of the battle.

It is not by accident that one of these books is titled *And the Lord Said Unto Satan*, because I felt I was face to face with the impossible contradiction and paradox of the presence of Evil in the world.

Here is how I pictured our life together before Nona went out and found her lesbian lover, Eva:

> ... they were like Chagall lovers ectoplasmically intertwined in a coupling of deep, resonating commonality ... there was a slight, playful, variable wind, the trees were rustling, the sun had gone down over the trees and houses on the other side of the street, the whole atmosphere was suffused with an expansive, cushioned sense of perfect tranquillity, more than that ... Joy ... Joie ... earthly, paradisal beatitude ...
> (p.261. The original manuscript of this "novel" is in Special Collections in the Michigan State University Library)

Then I ask, "What came into this perfect bliss and snapped its neck?" And the answer comes from the book of Job: "And the Lord said unto Satan, hast Thou considered my servant Job?"

The ending of *And the Lord Said Unto Satan* says it all:

> What was John of Patmos *on* when the angels came down from heaven and the beasts arose from the sea and he walked into the twelve-gated city and bathed in the river of the waters of life ... LET HIM THAT HATH UNDERSTANDING COUNT THE NUMBER OF THE BEAST, FOR IT IS THE NUMBER OF A MAN, AND HIS NUMBER IS SIX HUNDRED THREESCORE AND SIX ...

> And why, if there was any god anywhere at any time, why would he point The Raging Beast of Evil toward any house on any green hill bathed in the breezes of late Summer – **Hast thou considered my servant Job, there is none like him on the earth, a perfect and upright man.**

Even as I write these words now, I begin to feel malevolent 'presences' invade the yogic calm of my inner world. The battle of demons and angels is far from over. So-called 'modern man', separated from Total Reality by abstinence from the Sacred Drugs, sees only the visible manifestations of the invisible demonic-angelic war that rages all around us, but ask any Desaná or Kogi Indian in Colombia about the war of angels and demons and he will understand perfectly what you are talking about!

Christopher was taken away from us. In fact Nona and Eva and all three children moved back to Kansas City (where Nona was originally from) and only Alexandra, my second child with Nona, the middle child in our family, came back to visit and decided to stay and live with us.

Whatever equilibriums that had been established were destroyed again and Dette-Teresinha and I were thrown into turmoil – until somehow the 'gods' acted again, and I suddenly was given a grant by the Organization of American States to spend a year in the Atacama Desert in Chile doing archaeological research. By this time, of course, my classes at Michigan State were turned totally into research sessions centring around the place of Tiawanaku in the ancient world, and one day I had walked in and talked about why Tiawanaku was where it was because of its closeness to the Tropic of Capricorn:

"Certainly the primary 'identity' of Tiawanaku is found in its function as the House of the Sun, on, or close to the Tropic of Capricorn. The very TI in its name is written as a sun-glyph …"

Which I then proceeded to draw on the board:

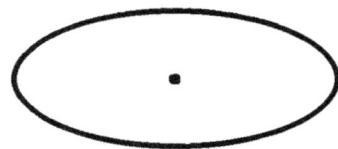

"The word 'Tiwat' in Luwian, the ancient language of Crete means 'sun,' and the Luwian phrase TIWATINAKU means 'The Young Lord Brings Life,' which is a coded message about the sun (the Young Lord) returning to life after his symbolic 'death' at the time of the Winter Solstice. The very centre of ancient theology was – very sensibly – the cyclic birth-death nature of the solar year. And Tiawanaku was the symbolic and ritual centre of ancient solar religion."

The next day I came in and before I had a chance to say a word a hand was raised in the back row.

"Tiawanaku is not *on* the Tropic of Capricorn. I fear you have misrepresented its location …"

"I never said it was *on* the Tropic," I answered, "the Tropic is 23° and Tiawanaku is at 19° … which I am very aware of," and then I made one of those statements that showed that although I had certainly grasped the fundamentals *vis a vis* Tiawanaku's place in ancient myth, there were still other pre-Tiawanakan realities that I had never even suspected in my wildest dreams but were important to understand in terms of still other dimensions of the place of the so-called "New" World in ancient world history and theology, "besides, there is really nothing of importance *on* the Tropic of Capricorn. It's just the Atacama Desert in Chile."

Before the next class began, the same student's hand (Kevin McNitt) went up again.

"It's not true that there's nothing of importance in the Atacama Desert in Chile. In fact a Belgian Jesuit named Gustave Le Paige spent most of his life there studying archaeological sites and he considers some sites, if I may quote, or at least paraphrase, 'the richest paleolithic sites in the world.'"

Then, after class, McNitt came up with a stack of books and a long bibliography of Le Paige's articles.

Most of the articles had been published in the reviews of two universities in Chile – the Catholic University in Santiago and the Universidad del Norte in Antofagasta – and I went over to the interlibrary loan office in the library here on campus and ordered everything. Then, once they arrived, I read all the articles and books, made notes, xeroxed maps and diagrams, and promptly applied for an Organization of American States/Pan American Union grant to go to the Atacama Desert itself and study the archaeological sites first hand.

I got the grant and a sabbatical from Michigan State and Alexandra decided to go with me. Dette-Teresinha couldn't come along because she had gone back into Medicine now and was in the middle of a residency in an area that suited her even more than surgery – Pathology itself ... the study of disease on a cellular level. From the beginning she took a special interest in Cytology, which, again, I felt was part of some larger plan for the New Millennium. Were the immortals themselves limited in space and time (the 'matter' with which and in which they had to exist) and beginning now to fight against their limitations on a cellular level?

We arrived in San Pedro de Atacama just after the Winter Solstice in the US, the Summer Solstice in South America. I would have almost one full year to wait before I could even hope to "put to the test" all the Stonehenge-like stone circles that I was certain were designed especially for Winter Solstice sightings, the time of the Winter Solstice, of course, being *the* death-rebirth centre of the whole year. Little could I realise that the timing had somehow been precisely planned. I had come when I was in a sense destined to come.

San Pedro itself was an oasis in the middle of a vast area that was now a desert but in earlier ages had been next to an inland sea that survived only as a few salt marshes (*salares*) here and there.

Alexandra was in her element. Somehow San Pedro had become a tourist Mecca and was filled with French, German, Israeli, Italian, Spanish, Japanese and English tourists. Little cafés had sprouted up facing on the main plaza and Alexandra installed herself at one of them and would sit all day sipping coffee and talking to tourists while I would go out on excursions into the desert.

We lived in a small *pensión*/boarding house and the landlady's son became very interested in me and what I was doing and he started going with me on my excursions. It was difficult to find Le Paige's places, though.

Le Paige talked about the Loma Negra, for example, a "butte" located at the intersection of the Puripica and Puritama rivers. No one had any idea where it was.

Before the Incas had invaded and dominated the Atacama Desert the people there had spoken a pre-Inca language called Kunza – which was supposed to be totally extinct. I wasn't entirely sure. I remembered back years before when Lucia and I had been helping Oscar Lewis (the author of *The Children of Sanchez*) transcribe tapes he had made by putting tape recorders in the homes of slum dwellers in Mexico City. Lucia and I could understand much of what was being said, but there were lots of words and expressions that neither of us could make heads or tails out of and I started transcribing the tapes phonetically, eventually going back into Nahuatl (Aztec) dictionaries and discovering much to our surprise that the words and expressions we couldn't understand weren't Spanish at all, but Nahuatl. There was a certain logic to the whole thing, of course. The Spaniards had come in as conquerors, destroyed the superstructure of the Aztec state, but the people themselves, subsisting in centuries of poverty, in a sense outside change and development, had retained their Aztec heritage. The lack of 'modern' education had enabled them to retain their native identity/language.

Was such a thing also possible with Kunza?

So I let it be known that I would pay anyone who could speak Kunza, let the word out among the 'people'. And as in all primitive societies, the word spread very quickly and within a week a very old man came knocking at my door. Very old and very poor.

He looked Japanese … or Korean … like a character out of an old Samurai film.

I remember sitting with him in the 'parlour' of the *pensión*, asking him:

"*Entonces, tu sabes hablar Kunza?*/So you speak Kunza?"

"*Puri* means water, *Puripica* is hot water, *Puritama* cold water," he answered.

"And?"

"That's it."

"OK," I answered and gave him ten dollars and he left saying something else I didn't understand and when I called him back and questioned him he told me "Oh, that's just goodbye in Kunza."

The irony was that the three words in Kunza that the old man had given me were exactly the words I needed.

The next day Keeno (the landlady's son) and I went back to a place which we had suspected might be the Loma Negra, a huge hump rising out of the desert, with two rivers cutting their way through gorges around its base. I put my hand in one of the rivers. It was warm. And the other was cold. The Puritama and Puripica, the Hot and Cold rivers, and the loma, the "rump" between the two, must have been the Loma Negra.

We climbed up to the top, saw evidence of archaeological digs. Probably Le Paige decades earlier. It was tough going. I saw a stone circle at the top, a solar-stellar clock; and from the top I could see other stone circles on other hills on the other side of the river thousands of feet below us. I couldn't help but be reminded of the Olduvai Gorge where Leaky had found some of his earliest human/humanoid remains, and wondered, if I had lowered myself down over the edge and looked at the jagged, exposed rock faces, might I not find a skull that went back a few million years. There was no reason why Man could not have evolved in the misnamed New World as well as in the misnamed Old World. After all some of the oldest dinosaur bones in the world had been found just a few thousand miles from where we were right now – in Argentina. Stone *bolas* (balls) identical to the ones used in slings by historic Argentinian Indians had been found in Argentina under geological deposits millions of years old.

Le Paige had said that the surface of the Loma Negra was literally littered with thousands of paleolithic pieces, that it was the richest paleolithic workshop find in the world. The new museum in San Pedro (with a giant apelike, larger than life bronze statue of Padre Le Paige out in front) was filled with scrapers and choppers and arrow- and spearheads. And the ground was still littered with more.

I was right *on* the Capricorn Point now.

My Atacama notebooks themselves have never been published, but in *Pulpsmith*, a Manhattan magazine I was on the staff of for years, I published an article in which I speculated that there had been "some sort of intercontinental paleolithic shared community of spiritual ideas that had designated the Americas as the central, sacred continent and had chosen the Atacama-Capricorn Point as *the central, sacred place of the ancient world, a place of pilgrimage, initiation, sacred drug-taking, enlightenment, rebirth."* ("Before Tiahuanaco," Vol.6, No.2, Summer 1986, p.120)

In an earlier article the year before (*Pulpsmith*, Vol.5, No.3, Autumn 1985) I had written about the fact that "at the 300,000 B.C. level in the Guadarrama mountains in central Spain ... there is an elephant burial with the bones arranged to form a T," and pointing to the rising sun at the time of the winter solstice. By the same token "in Neanderthal times at La Ferassie in the Dordogne a young child was buried under a limestone slab with 18 small pits hollowed out in it." (p.45)

The Mayas, basing their systems on ancient, prehistoric ideas, calculated the mathematical dimensions of the year beginning with the number 20 – our fingers and toes. *Uinac* in Maya is 'Man', *Uinal* is 'year'. And 18 is the 'magic' number that, multiplied by 20, gets as close to a solar year as it is possible without decimals/fractions – 360. It is not by accident that if you add up the numbers represented by the letters (in Hebrew every letter has a numerical equivalent) in the Hebrew word for life, C'HAI, it comes out to 18. The five days' difference between this man-based, life-based solar year and the true solar year of 365 days, for all pre-Columbian peoples were days of terror and madness when the universe itself was viewed as totally beserk and out of kilter.

What all this told me was that Man knew about the mathematics of the solstices as far back as 300,000 years ago so that choosing a place *on* the Tropic of Capricorn (the House of the Sun) as *the* sacred place or worship and pilgrimage, wasn't anything unexpected, but, on the contrary, just what you *would* have expected.

Although Le Paige, as far as I know, never actually says that the Atacama Desert was in constant contact with the Old World back to Paleolithic Times, his work is filled with drawings comparing pieces found in the Atacama and pieces from very ancient Old World sites in Europe, North Africa, the Middle East.

The implication is certainly there that there was a 'one-worldness' in ancient times that no one has ever even guessed at before. Paleolithic man was not landbound and isolated, but a constant traveller, an expert star-guided mariner.

As I point out in yet another article in *Pulpsmith* (Vol.6, No.1, Spring, 1986) "the ancients were obsessed with the idea of centre ... pivoting. The year pivoted around a certain solstice time-point, but they also wanted it to pivot around a certain point in space ... geography. Which is why they came up with the idea of *Itiwana* [the Zuñi equivalent of Tiawanaku], the Place in the Middle, or Mount Meru, the spine in the middle of the world ..." The ruins in the Atacama Desert, then, become "the original pre-Sumerian solstice temple and Tiahuanaco was built where it is for other aesthetic, astronomical reasons." (p.145)

A whole new dimension had suddenly opened up for me. The ancients, the immortals, had had a whole other world to themselves before they had moved to Tiawanaku. They had been in the Atacama Desert when it was lush and watery, and then when it had dried up, they had moved to Bolivia which in ancient times (given the extent of ancient irrigation projects that have been found in recent times) had been capable of supporting a hundred times more people than lived there now.

The immortals were flexible and mobile and (like Dette) capable of adaptations and radical, transcendent transformations.

I kept thinking of the local Indian names associated with Lake Titicaca/Tiawanaku:

Titi-Tata – Father of Tin
Inti kkaj-ja – Furnace of the Sun and his sons ...
Inti wiya – Immortal flame of the God-Sun and living light,
Thithi pata – the Island of the Cry, the universal scream,
Titi wiyana – Altar of tin to adore the Sun, our king,
Titi-kaka and Thithi-Ccotta – Tin-plated cup that contains all the waters reunited by the four winds of the Intis, Antilis or Andes ...

(Quoted in my article "The Voyage to the House of the Sun," *Pulpsmith*, Vol.1, No.1, Spring, 1982, pp.43-44)

It was obvious that the shift to a tin-centred mystique during the Bronze Age (the Anaku/Tin Lands of the Sumerians) had to some extent replaced the original heliocentrism of the sophisticated sun-worshippers who had inhabited the Atacama Desert.

Now here I was back at the beginnings of the beginnings.

"I hate to leave," said Keeno standing on the top of Loma Negro surveying the desert below us that stretched out to the horizons around us.

"Me too," I admitted, "but it is getting late."

Something wanted to keep us there forever.

But it *was* getting late and we had to leave, and when we got to the bottom of the slope that we had climbed up on, there was an old man waiting there for us, wearing a poncho and *gorro*, one of those Andean woven or knit caps with flaps coming down over the ears, the same kind of cap that I'd seen over and over again on stone reliefs in ancient Turkey, a shepherd's crook in his hand, surrounded by a herd of llamas and alpacas.

At first I was a little startled to see anyone out here in the middle of all this vast emptiness. I mean it was a little crazy to be going around the way we were, as if the vast world around us were all just user friendly, benign, harmless. We carried no weapons, were totally defenceless against whatever might swoop down out of the skies upon us.

But the old man seemed harmless enough.

"*Ven conmigo*/Come with me," he said eccentrically and motioned for us to follow him over to an old stone hut close to the bank of the Puripica River.

It was a strange lunar landscape. I could see snow-covered peaks in the distance, undoubtedly the source of the cold water in the cold-water river.

I looked at Keeno as if to ask "Should we go along with him?"

And he nodded as if to say, "Yeah, it's OK..."

And we went into what looked like a stone hut/house that had somehow survived from very ancient times. It wasn't 'inca', though, large, perfectly cut and fitted stones, but more rustic, improvised. Pre-Inca ... only how far back might the 'pre' have gone?

There was a thatched roof, a bed on the stone block floor, a couple of chairs, and a table full of artifacts.

"*Te quiero dar todo*/I want to give you everything," said the wrinkled old man, looking right through me with his solemn, penetrating eyes that reminded me of cases of severe depression, a solemnity that allowed no light or hope in but that viewed everything in a tragic, hopeless light.

My daughter Cecilia, my second child of my first marriage, by now almost thirty, was a paranoid-schizophrenic in the mental health system in Michigan and often I'd go down to the clinic/half-way house where she had lunch every day and so I had had lots of first-hand experience with mental cases over the last few years.

This old man looked like a real 'case' to me. But maybe he wasn't.

Transculturally someone who looked like a case in one social setting might be perfectly normal in another. Look at myself. In occidental terms I was a crazy hearing voices, but in ancient shamanistic terms, I was a holy man in contact with a very real spirit world.

"*No puedo acceptar tus cosas asi*/I can't take your things just like that," I answered, looking down at the objects on the table, stone scrapers, hatchets, a mortar and pestle ... much the same types of things we had seen scattered all over the ground up on top of the Loma Negra.

"I insist!" the old man said with just a rumble of anger in his tone and manner.

"Take them!" Keeno urged me.

He was the 'native' around here and I went along with his urgings, reached into my pocket and took out the wad of bills that I always carried with me, tried to hand the money to the old man. Only he scornfully refused to touch the money, as if it were contaminated, dirty.

"What use is money to me here?" he asked, looking around at the walls of his house and, by implication, the limits of his entire world/existence.

It reminded me of one time years before when I was being driven across the Bolivian *altiplano* from La Paz to Potosí where I was to give a lecture on contemporary American painting and literature (under USIS – US Information Service – sponsorship).

I had seen a little boy standing next to the road crying and I'd told my driver to stop and had got out and instantly started shivering in the cold Andean wind. The little boy was wearing short trousers, a rag of a cotton shirt and was barefoot, mucous streaming out of his nose, screaming "*Thanta, thanta, thanta.*" Which I didn't understand. My driver translated for me: "Bread ... he wants bread." I reached into my pocket and took out my usual wad, peeled off a couple of bills, but he wouldn't take them. "Why won't he take the money?" I asked my driver. "Look around you!" he said. We were a hundred miles from La Paz. It was all desolate wasteland. Beyond wasteland ... total emptiness.

And it was the same here in the Atacama Desert, wasn't it. The same, if not worse.

I took my watch off my wrist. I felt I had to give him something ... the jaguars inside my head all agitated and 'crazy' now, howling as if to try to tell me something, only I couldn't make out exactly what, some moment of maximum excitement for them.

About what? Why?

"Que interés tengo en el tiempo?" he said to me, pushing my hand with the watch in it away, "What interest do I have in time? What do Time and I have to do with each other?"

And he reached up under his poncho and took out a long spear-point and suddenly thrust it toward me so quickly and violently that Keeno grabbed my arm and pulled me back away from him.

"What are you afraid of, that I will cut your heart out and sacrifice it to the gods?" he laughed, handing me the point, "just another present ..." then looking down at the floor, the 'interview' was over, "*es tiempo de despedirnos* ... it's time to say goodbye ..."

I could hardly think at all, my mind-jaguars were in such a mad whirl, the noise inside my head so loud that I almost expected everyone else to hear it, as if it threatened to break out beyond the confines of my skull.

Keeno motioned for me to leave.

I took the spear point and the other objects, put them in the pockets of my Harris tweed jacket that over the years had served me well in the cold airlessness of the high Andes. And we backed out the door as if we were leaving the presence of some ancient emperor, backing out of the sanctuary of some lost Holy of Holies.

"Boy, I'm glad to get out of there," said Keeno.

"Just some old llama shepherd," I said, but not believing what I was saying. He wasn't just some old llama shepherd, but... but what...? I couldn't put my finger on what or who he really was.

We got in the car and were half way back to San Pedro when suddenly I remembered. That ancient semitic face, the large nose, the wrinkles, that expression of menacing sullenness. Of course ... it was the face of Huehueteotl, Tatawari, Old Grandfather Fire ...

"Stop, we've got to go back!" I shouted at Keeno. "He was one of The Ancients, the Old Fire God ... we've got to go back!"

"Not me! Not for the world!" he said and kept driving.

Not very fast. After all it was a dirt road filled with potholes, hardly a road at all.

I opened the door and was about to jump out and take my chances when he braked and gave in.

"I must be just as crazy as all the rest of you ... what do you mean 'the Old Fire God'?"

"It's my second 'epiphany,'" I explained, "First was the woman I am now married to who couldn't/didn't want to come with me on this trip ... perhaps for reasons I can't even guess at ... and now the Old Fire God." I stopped, tried to collect and organise my thoughts and emotions, thinking we should have taken a picture, pictures don't lie, something to compare with the innumerable ceramic sculptures of the Old Fire God from ancient times, sculptures which I had *always* believed were portraits of a real god-man, the jaguars inside me howling that I shouldn't make the revelation I was about to make, howling which I ignored and simply said what I felt I had to, "at one time there were men who walked this earth who, I don't know how, eventually 'became gods.' There is a way to alter the biochemistry of death and mortality and they discovered it. They became 'immortal' and created a whole sacral world around them, perhaps first here in the Atacama Desert, certainly later at Tiawanaku which in the entire ancient world was known as the Home of the Gods. As long as they eat the Apples of Immortality, the 'thorn-apples' That Make Old Men Young Again talked about in the Sumerian epic *Gilgamesh*, the apples tended by the goddess Freya in Teutonic myth, the fruit of the Tree of Good and Evil in Genesis ... they would never die ... and the face of that old man back there was the face of one of the immortals ... I'd stake my life on it ... they can assume different forms ... it's one of the basic tenets in Hindu myth, the idea of multiple forms or avatars ... they're telepathic ... they can change form ... transcend space ... and I believe they are trying to 'come back.'"

"In what sense?" Keeno turning the car around and starting back toward the Loma Negra which we could soon see, a huge black hump on the horizon.

"Geopolitically," I answered, "some sort of 'second coming.' The New Earth ..."

"You mean Jesus was one of them?" asked Keeno.

I instantly thought of not merely the Resurrection but the Assumption ... the bodily entrance of the Virgin Mary into Heaven.

"Could be ..."

"I used to be a Catholic," he said as we moved back through the slowly settling clouds of dust that we had stirred up when we'd been coming the other way, "but then I gradually drifted away from it all. It all seemed so unreal for me, the Resurrection, the Second Coming ... but now ..."

Ten minutes more and we were back to the old man's stone hut. Keeno stopped, we got out and ...

"There's no roof," he said.

And it was true. The hut was still there but looked like it hadn't been lived in for thousands of years. No sign of the old man or his llamas. It was as if nothing that had happened had really happened.

I reached into my pockets expecting them to be empty – and they were ... except for the artifacts we had picked up on the Loma Negra itself, *and the one spear-point that the old man had pulled out from under his poncho at the very end of our visit.*

I pulled it out and showed it to Keeno.

"This is all that's left to prove any of it ever happened."

He stood still and shook his head, closed his eyes.

"Are we really here now or back in San Pedro asleep? I haven't eaten any San Pedro cactus for years."

"But you *have* eaten it?"

He nodded, eyes open, back to normal again.

"Unfortunately yes."

So, in a sense, he was one of 'us.' And everything that had happened had happened in jaguar-shaman hyperspace, that other dimension that the sacred drug(s) open up, inhabited by beings that appear to the rest of the world only in dreams.

I kept thinking of Vishnu who, in Hindu myth, is said to live with the rest of the gods on Mount Meru (Tiawanaku). He sleeps on the back of the Eternity Snake, Ananta, the Hindu mythological equivalent of the dragon in the Greek versions of the story, the serpent who eats the thorn-apple in *Gilgamesh*, the serpent in the Garden in Genesis. Vishnu, in this context, is the equivalent of the sun-god in Greek myth. And he is said to dream all of reality and when he wakes from his dream all of the reality he has dreamed disappears. So we are all the dreamstuff of Vishnu's dreaming mind. What had happened with my encounter with the Old Fire God was that something 'real' had somehow made itself out of Dreamtime into my hands.

Or there might be another explanation.

We had drunk water out of the Puripica River. We hadn't brought any water with us and were totally dehydrated when we had come down from the Loma Negra, just before the old llama shepherd had appeared. Could the water itself have had psychedelic properties that had then simulated a collective hallucination in both of us?

And the spear point that I was convinced had been given to me by the Old Fire God. Couldn't it have merely been another spear point that I had picked up on the Loma Negro? I had been talking to Keeno a lot about the Old Fire God and other ancient gods during the preceding week. Could that have been the raw material out of which our shared hallucination (if it was really that) had been generated?

Let me get ahead of my story a little here and recount what that one surviving spear point had to tell me. When I got back to Michigan State I started haunting the library again, determined to place that particular spear point in its true historical setting.

I made a point of using facsimile editions and after about two weeks of frantic searching, one day I found a spear point that exactly matched the one from the Atacama Desert. I placed the Atacama point on top of the one in the book and it fitted exactly. There was even a little 'break' at the proximal end of the Atacama point that exactly matched a 'break' in the facsimile in the book I was matching it up with.

The same shape, same size, same flaking patterns on the blade edge ... and 'broken' in exactly the same place in exactly the same way.

The origin of the blade that so exactly matched my Atacama piece? It was from the Negev Desert in Israel and bore the date 60,000 B.C. Which told me, didn't it, that there had been communication between the Middle East and South America even back on the 60,000 B.C. level. The Atacama Desert had been the House of the Sun at least as far back as 60,000 B.C.

And as I am taking a break in the narrative anyhow, let me tell you about another strange encounter Alexandra and I had in Santiago de Chile on our way back to the US.

Another 'coincidence' that somehow seems very intentionally planned.

We had got a room in a *pensión* named Londres and one day I was in the lounge having my afternoon coffee with Alex when a bearded, bustling German came in and sat down and we got talking to him.

"Where are you from in Germany?" I asked.

"Munich."

"And you're ... ?" asked Alexandra.

"If I may say so in all modesty, the world's greatest expert in prehistoric points."

"Oh," I said, "let me show you something I have in my suitcase," and I went and got the point that the Old Fire God had given me.

He looked at it with critical distrust.

"Something from Germany?" he asked, "France? The Middle East? It's typically Mousterian."

"No, it's from the Atacama Desert!" I answered, and Herr Doktor Professor got all bustling and defensive.

"No, it can't be, it must be a fraud!"

"Tata Wari's fraud?" I smiled.

"Who? What?"

Of course he didn't have the slightest sense of comparative New and Old World anything. They never do. If they did they would have seen the same things that I saw. The whole theory of the exclusive peopling of the New World across the Bering Strait is totally based on ignorance.

"The Old Fire God!"

"I don't know what you're talking about."

"I'm quite aware of that, although he is portrayed on the Metternich Stela in Vienna – as the Old Sun God," I answered, and the minute I said that I realised that I had just answered a question that had been bothering me for a long, long time about whether or not there was any sort of equivalence between the Old Fire God and the Old Sun God. There was. He was the same person. Fire was sun and sun was fire.

The Metternich Stela was a large Egyptian stone stele all full of chiselled-out figures and hieroglyphs, and at the very top was a representation of the Old Sun God who was exactly the same as the Old Fire God that filled Pre-Columbian pots ... the Old Fire God who had given me my Mousterian point from the remote world of 60,000 B.C.

All right... so much for a disruption in the narrative, let's go back to the Atacama Desert again, just after I had been given the ancient stone spear-point.

The next day I was talking to Keeno's mother's boyfriend who didn't live in the *pensión* but just a few streets over toward the main plaza. He was a retired mining engineer and spent most of his time in the patio of the *pensión* sitting around drinking coffee, listening to the radio and reading the newspaper.

I was sitting there looking at some Phoenician inscriptions I had transcribed from the *Revue d'Assyriologie*, frustrated, as always, by the fact that in the Phoenician materials actually translated into English I had never found any equivalent of the myth about travelling across the ocean to the New World/Land of the Sun King and I felt that among the hundreds and hundreds of *untranslated* pages in the *Revue d'Assyriologie*, there must be references to such a voyage.

Cyrus Gorden in his *Riddles in History* (New York, 1974) had, so to speak, put his stamp of approval on a Phoenician inscription that had been found in Brazil talking about mariners who had been blown off course during the reign of Hiram of Tyre and who had landed in Brazil which matched up beautifully with the account in the second Book of Kings in the bible about the pact made between the Phoenician king Hiram of Tyre and King Solomon to team up on a sailing venture to go to Ophir to get gold.

Up to now no one had any idea of exactly where Ophir was, but if some of the ships had been blown off course and landed in Brazil, it seemed reasonable that they had been on their way to South America in the first place, not Brazil, but... perhaps Tiawanaku.

Years earlier in La Paz, the brilliant scholar Mario Montaño Aragón had taken me to a museum and showed me a pot that was filled with what was obviously a very early form of Phoenician script, the kind of script that would have been used at the time of Solomon somewhere around the 1,000 B.C. level.

Now a whole new revelation was about to take place in my life *vis a vis* the Phoenician presence in the New World.

Señor Gutierrez (Pepe) came in and looked down at my notebook filled with Phoenician writing and said "I've seen exactly those same letters before. At Punto del Sol in the south of Chile. We were doing some petroleum explorations, and a friend of mine found a cache of stone dishes with those same letters carved on them. I remember very well ... letters like this one ... shaped like the number five." And he pointed at a Phoenician 'L':

That, indeed, did look like the number 5.

"The Indians down there say that Solomon walked in those mountains," pointing to the mountains in the distance, "and they say that the mountains there are filled with gold ... although I don't know of anyone who has ever explored them for gold."

Solomon andaba en estos montañas – Solomon walked in those mountains.

Those were his very words. And without knowing about the reference in I Kings 9:

> King Solomon also built a fleet of ships at Ezion-Geber, which is near Eloth on the shore of the Sea of Reeds in the land of Edom. Hiram sent servants of his with the fleet, mariners who were experienced on the sea, to serve with Solomon's men. They came to Ophir; there they obtained gold in the amount of four hundred and twenty talents, which they delivered to King Solomon.
>
> (*Tanakh: A New Translation of the Holy Scriptures*, Jewish Publication Society, 1985, p.537.)

I should explain that the Sea of Reeds referred to here is the correct translation of what is usually referred to as the Red Sea.

Could it have been possible that Solomon himself had come to the New World with Hiram's mariners – and actually been in Southern Chile?

Seeing that the Atacama Desert had been in contact with the Middle East as far back as 60,000 B.C. and that Tiawanaku was already known as Anaku, the Tin-Lands, in 3,000 B.C., and that Quechua was essentially the same as Sanskrit from India, it seemed unlikely to me that all 'real-time' knowledge of the existence and nature of the New World was lost by 3,000 B.C. Especially seeing that the Phoenicians (as Herodotus says) themselves had originated in the area of the Persian Gulf, just below Iraq, the location of ancient Sumer and the Sumerians.

Certainly Jewish folklore was filled with stories about Solomon's miraculous ability to travel to any place in the world in an instant, and later I was to discover all sorts of stories about Solomon and the stars that sounded very much like a Jewish version of the zodiac stories/twin myths that had served as star-charts to get ancient mariners to the New World.

I tried to find the dishes that Pepe had told me about, and actually did find the wife of the man who had found the dishes (out in the middle of the desert in a mining camp) but he was working in Antofagasta and I never could locate him. Maybe he didn't want to be found. There were strong laws in Chile against 'stealing' ancient objects and in the mid-eighties, when I was there, Chile was under the power of a strong military dictatorship. It was very dangerous to have found and kept ancient stone dishes from the middle of the Chilean desert.

But the stories all seemed to match up, the voyages to Ophir, the inscriptions in Brazil (and Bolivia), the stories about Solomon in the Southern Chilean desert. The Old World and New World sources matched up – undoubtedly Solomon *had* come to the New World and had been to Chile.

I began to notice the uncanny similarities between certain pots from the Atacama Desert and pots from Troy III – on the 3,000 B.C. level (see page 45).

Troy, after all, was in Turkey, just above Mesopotamia. If the Mesopotamians in 3,000 B.C. based their epics on stories of voyaging to Anaku/Tiawanaku, why shouldn't the Trojans at the same time have also voyaged to the New World?

The longer we stayed in San Pedro, the more convinced I became that I was living in one of the great sacred areas of ancient times. It got so that I couldn't even sleep at night but would get up and go out into the courtyard of our *pensión* and stand for hours watching the stars parade across the sky. Having spent most of my life at sea level in cloudy (or smoggy) areas, I had never really experienced the reality of the heavens the way I was experiencing it now.

It was so bright that you could read a newspaper by starlight. There were stars that I had never seen before. It wasn't just a star here and there in the blackness, but ropes of stars, an almost continuous blanket of light interspersed with a little blackness here and there.

At first I would call Dette on the primitive car-battery-powered phone in the local post office. There was no electricity at all during the day in San

Pedro, only two hours of generator-powered electricity in the evening. So they had to use a car battery to run the one phone in town.

But then, during my hours following the stars across the heavens, seeing Herakles kill the Crab (Cancer), kill the Nemean Lion (Leo), the Hopi twins kill the Flint Monster (again our Leo, the Hindu Lunar Mansion of the knife), the origins of all the episodes of all the ancient myths spread out right before me, we would begin to communicate telepathically.

"*Agora voce esta conosco*/Now you are with us ..." she told me one night, her presence soft and furry and shimmering all around me.

"*Que pena que não estamos juntos*," I answered, "What a shame we aren't together."

"*Mas somos!*" she said, her presence so strong that she almost incarnated right there in my arms, not just telepathy but teleincarnation.

And it was true, her presence never left, not at night, not during the day, never ...

"*Voltaré dentro de pouco*," I said to her one night, "I'll be coming back soon ..."

"*Não tan pronto que voce acha* – not as soon as you think. First you have to go to Bolivia and enter into the heart of ... what do you think it is ... darkness ... or eternal light."

"You mean the caves?" I asked.

"*Que bruto e o homen moderno*," she said bitterly, "how stupid modern man is ... *eli acha que sabe tudo y não sabe nada*. He thinks he knows everything and he doesn't know anything."

I agreed, and wondered, was I the first to step inside the one-worldness of The Ancients, or were there others like me? Was I the first to live inside the knowledge of the ancient voyages across the oceans to the Home of the Gods, the first to understand the place of ancient South America in ancient myth and reality, the first to couple with one of the immortals themselves?

I didn't really want to leave the Atacama Desert. There was a sense of sacred specialness in the very air we breathed, the ground we trod ... and there were a thousand stories that I would like to have followed up on. I wanted to go to the Punto del Sol itself and walk in the mountains where Solomon had walked. There were rumours, myths, legends about tombs out in the Atacama Desert itself, huge carefully worked slabs covering the entrances of cave-tombs, other stories about pathways up to the tops of mountains where there were 'cities' like Machu Picchu, stories about stone igloos in the middle of the desert where the "dwarfs" had lived ...

There was enough material to investigate for many lifetimes, but in a sense I had already received my 'orders' from Dette – it was time to return to Bolivia.

I had all sorts of misgivings. In the high desert of Atacama I functioned fine, but when I went up higher into Bolivia, fifteen thousand feet up and more, I began to get vague, my heart overworked, I couldn't sleep at all. I was in my late fifties now, totally out of shape. It had already been difficult for me to climb up to places like Loma Negra, would I even (in spite of all the San Pedro cactus that I found readily available around me) survive a trip to the foothills of Mount Illimani where I knew the entrance was to what I had begun to be convinced was the Cave-World of the Immortals?

I had already written to my old friends Mariano and Carmen Baptista in La Paz when I had first got my grant from the Organization of American States. They already knew I was in the Atacama Desert. Now I called them and asked if they were in the mood for visitors.

"Of course," said Carmen, "we always love to see you."

And she meant it.

We couldn't have been closer. I had first met the Baptistas in Caracas when I was there between 1964 and '66 when Mariano had been in 'exile,' so to speak, because of his involvement as Secretary to Paz Estenssoro during Estessoro's dictatorship. Not that Mariano was one of the bad guys. His grandfather had been president of Bolivia. He was from "that class," that upper strata that ruled Bolivia. The dictator had been thrown out, then there had been a time of reaction against everything he represented. The political pendulum had swung another swing, and now Mariano was back in politics, this time as Secretary of Education.

Carmen was a painter. Very successful. In fact most of the money in the family now came from her. I had bought a couple of pictures from her when we were in Caracas together and my favourite was a picture of a Bolivian miner and his wife having lunch in the middle of a mine itself – in one of the tin mines in Anaku, the (Sumerian) Tin-Lands. It hung over a hand carved credenza from Mexico next to my mother's Mexican silver in the dining room.

Alexandra didn't want to leave at all.

"Let's just stay here forever. You could teach English and write. We don't need much to live on."

"If I lived on my writing," I told her, "I wouldn't have to worry about dieting. And who here wants to learn English? We haven't seen one American since we've been here." Although we had seen some Australians and English.

So we both rather reluctantly left Atacama, a leave-taking full of tears and promises to keep in touch with all the people we had come to love, and took a bus to Calama where we caught an all-night train to La Paz.

The train-ride to La Paz was one of the strangest nights either of us had ever spent in our lives.

The Bolivian trains were relics out of the nineteenth century. Originally from England, they had been in continuous service for well over a century. They had been maintained mechanically, but the seats, the toilets, all the little amenities that made a long train ride bearable, had gone to ruin.

And there were little hands that kept delving into my pockets in the dark so that I really couldn't sleep. Indians (especially Indian women) everywhere, sitting on the floor in the corridors, in every corner. Wall to wall. No lights. These little hands creeping into my pockets like hungry squirrels.

I wasn't angry. These descendents of the great races of the ancient world, these latter-day Anatolians (Turks), Sumerians (Iraqis), Indus Valley peoples ... for centuries had been oppressed, ignored, totally marginalised.

When a hand would slither into my pocket I simply would take it out and give it a soft little slap as if to say "Naughty, naughty, putting your hands in other people's pockets isn't right."

I wasn't outside, but very much *inside* their mystique and world-view. My internal jaguars spent the night purring. They 'knew' I was home, inside the nest of the Holy Ancients who had survived into the twentieth century and whose entire world was about to take flight at the turning of the millennium.

They slowly seemed to understand who and what I was, that I was some sort of furry-souled messenger/angel who was somehow inside their world-view; and eventually the hands stopped violating my privacy, we all bonded and became a common soul. I slept for a while, all bundled up in a wool poncho I had bought in San Pedro. We were slowly moving up on to the Bolivian high plain (*altiplano*). I could feel the air begin to thin out, my heart begin to overwork. The Indians who had lived here for thousands of years, of course, had actually developed large chests, huge lungs, adapted to the thinner air. Evolution was a continuous ongoing process working from generation to generation. The infants with the largest lung capacities survived and grew up to marry others with large lung capacities. Thousands of years of unconscious, automatic selective breeding had been going on and the Indians all around me in the darkness were the survivors. Sea-level peoples like the Spaniards came into this

Himalayan ambience and did very badly. I remembered Mariano Baptista telling me years before, on another visit to La Paz: "We, the Europeans, seldom survive beyond sixty, sixty-five." With my system energized by the San Pedro cactus that I had been eating, though, I suffered much less than I had on earlier, previous trips when I was not so continuously tied in to the sacred drugs of immortality.

And our stay in Atacama had been helpful too. It wasn't an abrupt change from sea level up to the clouds, but a slow ascent over a period of months and months.

Then some time around midnight, the train stopped and backed into a siding.

"*Que esta aconteciendo?*/What's happening?" I asked the old woman on the floor next to me.

"*Siempre es asi, quedamos aca casi todo la noche*/It's always this way, we stay here almost all night."

Why? One of those forever-unanswered questions.

I got up.

"What's happening?" asked Alexandra.

She was only twelve at the time, totally intrepid, fearless.

"Let's move around a little."

I wasn't worried about leaving the baggage. Let them have what they wanted. I had the ancient spear-point that Tata Wari, the Old Fire-God had given me, wrapped in a piece of suede tied around my neck. It was my own magic amulet, my gift from the gods. Besides, I felt, we had come to some sort of 'oneness,' hadn't we; we had all begun to see ourselves as part of the same tribe travelling on the same time-tracks from a common psychic past.

"OK," said Alex and we got up, made our way slowly through the mass of bodies sprawled all over the carriage, stepped outside into the cold, roaring night.

There was some sort of station up ahead in the darkness and in front of the station a giant bonfire surrounded by hundreds of Indians.

"I'm scared," said Alex, "let's go back into the train."

"Nothing to be afraid of," I reassured her, and I took her arm and together we walked toward the fire, as we approached feeling that somehow I was moving into a common psychoplasmic flow, the faces of the Indians standing around the fire, dancing, or simply staring, all feline, the air filled with music, someone playing a *charango*, a kind of ukulele made out of the body of an Andean hairy armadillo, someone else playing a drum, another musician playing a *guena*, a flute made out of a human thighbone, strangely vigorous *huinos*, music out of dreams ... or nightmares.

As we approached, faces turned toward us, at first distrustful, even fearful, but when our psychoplasms touched and intertwined, the jaguar faces smiled and the eyes were full of welcome instead of rejection.

We were home.

Perhaps I should never have allowed Alexandra to take the sacred, mind- and soul-altering cactus when Keeno and I and other Indians would go out into the desert at night and have Atacama Cactus fests, sitting around a fire like this and communing with the night, the Allpast, Allpresent, Allfuture, the omnipresent Allgods singing in the etherised night that slumbered around us.

But I had.

Back in East Lansing she had been experimenting with the usual teenage drugs that were circulating around, but in San Pedro I had, rightly or wrongly, decided to let her come into the World of the Immortals. Why should I partake of eternal life, the Communion of Immortality, and leave her stranded in time?

Later, when Nona forced her to come back to Kansas and had separated her from Sacral Time/Timelessness, these sacred drug sessions would have their toll. She would develop panic-attacks and agoraphobia. Which was totally understandable in the horrific secularism of any modern city filled with hungry, random violence.

But now, in the joyous, howling *altiplano* night, surrounded by fellow jaguar-shamans, an entire shamanistic *race*, I had never seen her more at ease, self-fulfilled, beatific.

They danced and she danced with them, the air filled with a strange mix of growls and music.

We were totally accepted. Some of the Indian women had followed us out of the train and I had started dancing with one of them, young, beautiful, a woman who could have flown to Pakistan and disappeared into the streets of Karachi and no one would have ever asked her for a passport, an obvious descendent of the Proto-Indo-Mediterranean race. And as I was dancing, a rooster-chicken dance, blatantly and shamelessly sexual, a bi-polar psychological wrestling match between *macho* (male) and *embra* (female), slowly the 'stranger' (*inconnu*) became an old friend, DetteTeresinha *there*, reincarnated in the body in front of me.

They understood who I was – who we were – and in fact, I wondered, was this the way these sacred people survived, in a sense 'disguised' as Indians, assuming a false socio-economic identity in this society that had been handed down from colonial times? Survived by wearing false-face masks and playing roles that totally hid what they really were – the Immortals themselves?

If I had looked up and seen Tata Wari, the Old Fire God himself, playing the flute or beating on a drum, I would not have been surprised. If Siva, Vishnu, Parvati, Yama, Kubera, Ganesa, elephant-head and all, had suddenly emerged out of the night into the light, I would not have been surprised. I knew where I was, we all knew where and who we were – this was the suburbs of heaven and we were the travelling gods in disguise.

Some time not long before dawn, the train started up again and they blew the old nineteenth century steam whistle and Alex said "We'd better get back on the train."

Everyone hurrying now, the Walpurgisnacht, Night on Bald Mountain, finished, a Witch's Sabbat that was really a convention of the gods.

We got back into our seats and lurched into movement, on our way again; and it couldn't have been more than an hour later when the sky lightened and the sun, more brilliant than I had ever seen it, blazed up on the horizon. As we moved closer to La Paz I began to see familiar shapes all over the dry hills, stone ruins here and there, a tower, a 'gate' similar to the sun-gate at Tiawanaku:

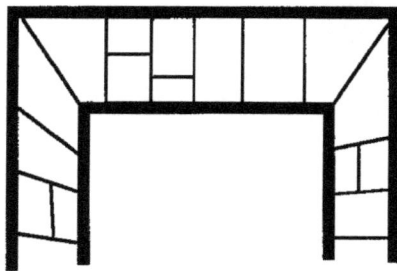

The same sorts of stone structures that you find throughout the South Seas – another one of the routes from Asia (the Indus Valley) to the New World. * There were a hundred years of archaeology still to be done, not just in the Tiawanaku area but throughout the Bolivian *altiplano*.

We had to transfer to a bus at one point in Oruru, in the middle of the Bolivian copper country, a place where you'd see beehive-shaped ovens like the smelters of ancient Asia Minor all over the landscape.

Oruru. It was just a different way of spelling the ancient Sumerian word *ururu* – to smelt. **

We were coming 'home' now, home to the fields of the Gods, home to the territory of the Old Fire God where the very act of smelting was sacred magic. As we approached La Paz Alexandra brightened up.

"It's wonderful, isn't it," she said, reaching for words to express her emotions, "it's like ... I don't know ... coming home ..."

Matching exactly what I had already been feeling for a long time.

When we came in, Mariano was waiting for us.

"*Que tal, viejo, Ustedes parecen medio muertos. Es un viaje bien duro!* How you doing, old guy. You both look half dead, it's a long trip!" he said, giving us both *abrazos*, helping us get our stuff into the car, and within a few minutes we were up in the hills overlooking La Paz in the Baptista mansion. In fact in order to get into the area itself you had to pass by a military checkpoint. Bolivia was ruled by a small, mostly white minority and the country itself was a vast mass of poor 'Indians' excluded from practically everything. There was no such thing as Operation Headstart. In Bolivia, for the Indians it was Operation No Start since the Spanish Conquista in the sixteenth century.

But you hardly thought about class wars and millennial injustices once you were inside the Baptista mansion.

Carmen made lots of money as a painter and the money always went into the house. She'd build on another wing or another storey, add another corridor connecting Block A to Block B and turn it into a picture-filled gallery.

There were all sorts of little 'touches' here and there. Like in the central patio (whose origin, in Spain, ultimately was the Roman atrium, dating back to the times when Spain was the Roman province of Iberia) where she had had a false door built into one wall and then had sculpted and painted a Bolivian woman standing in the doorway, the bottom part of the door closed, the top open ... so that when you first came into the patio you really believed that someone was standing there.

Alexandra, an artist herself already even at twelve, got a big kick out of it. Got the giggles.

"It really fooled me. I should have known better, but it's so realistic!"

---

* See A. Riesenfeld's *The Megalithic Culture of Melanesia*. Leiden: E.J. Brill, 1950. Riesenfeld is especially helpful because besides talking about megalithic ruins, he also deals with myth so that the connections are doubly confirmed.

** See Franz Kocher's article "Ururu (Am Feur) Dorren," in *Studies in Honor of Benno Landsberg, Assyriological Studies*, No.16, Chicago: The Oriental Institute of the U. of Chicago, 1965, p.323 ff.

Carmen's mother was living with her, an old German from Southern Germany, widowed now for twenty-five years, her husband, Carmen's father, assassinated during a play for political power a quarter of a century earlier.

Carmen herself was the most beautiful woman I had ever seen, black hair and eyes, perfect white skin. She had spent a good part of her childhood in Washington when her father had been the Bolivian ambassador to the US, and her English was perfect.

"*Hugo*," she gushed as we came in, giving me a big hug, her English deserting her for a moment, "*que bueno verte* – it's so good to see you! And Alexandra!" hugging her too, "you two must be starved. Let's get your stuff in your room and then I've got a nice lunch waiting for you."

We followed her into our little 'apartment' off to the side of the house.

There was a huge bathroom with a Jacuzzi right in the middle, two huge beds in the bedroom, a monster-sized TV with a built-in VCR and hundreds of video-tapes, all carefully labelled.

"It's all BBC. I used to tape all kinds of programmes when we were in England. Remember, a few years ago, before we came back to La Paz?"

"Sure," I lied. Things I should have remembered but didn't. There had been long years when we had hardly remained in contact at all, maybe a Christmas card, a few lines here and there, a birthday phonecall. In fact I vaguely remembered calling London.

The walls were filled with Carmen's 'indigenous' paintings, pictures that looked like they had been painted by totally untutored native artists, purposefully crude, childlike, naïve.

Lucia, my first wife, had kept all of Carmen's 'primitive' pictures and I'd taken the 'normal,' three-dimensional ones with me when we'd broken up. Lucia's whole house in East Lansing, in fact, was like one vast museum of indigenous folk-art – a good place for Carmen's paintings that portrayed things like the Bolivian devil-dancers with their devil-masks, demons from the mines ... the underworld.

"So how was Chile?" Carmen asked me after we have got our bags stashed away in our rooms, walking down a tiled corridor to the dining room.

"I didn't want to leave," said Alexandra who had immediately warmed to Carmen, "I wanted to just stay there forever. I could have done portraits of tourists or paintings of ruins and things and sold them to tourists, and Dad could have taught English."

"Why not!" said Carmen, "the more structureless the better."

"You certainly don't practice what you preach!" I answered.

"Who ever does?" she laughed as we walked into the dining room, a big bowl of creamy pasta-noodles in the centre, filled with bits of ham and salami. Black beans. Black bread, a plate heaped full with chirimoyas and mangos.

I could see a huge chirimoya tree in the patio, its top-heavy tentacular branches supported by Y-shaped wooden supports.

"Home-grown chirimoyas!" I said.

My favourite fruit. Called *nonas* in Brazil. A taste like a very sweet Bartlett pear, but the fruit itself in cells, or segments, each segment with a huge black seed.

Carmen's mother already sitting, waiting for us.

I gave her a hug. We were the best of friends. She reminded me of my old Czech grandmother. Carmen's mother was someone I was very comfortable with. Being with her was almost like taking a time-trip back to Cicero with my grandmother.

The food was great. A little wine hit the spot.

"*Aber bist du nicht müde?*/But aren't you tired?" Carmen's mother asked me.

"*Ich wollte eine woche schlafen!*/I could sleep a week," I said, as she switched over into Spanish for Alex, "*Cansada?*"

Alex kind of surprising me, answering "*Muy cansada!*"

Of course she'd picked up all kinds of Spanish. It was one of those things that happened automatically.

"So ... Mario Montaña Aragón wants to see you tomorrow afternoon," said Mariano, "he has a new book he wants to show you."

The author of *Raíces Semíticas en la Religiosidad Aymara y Kichua – Semitic Roots in Quechua and Aymara Religiosity*. Someone else (besides me) who saw all the old links between the Andes and the semitic/Proto-Indo-Mediterranean world.

"Great!"

"And then on Wednesday Carlos Ponce Sanginés wants to talk to you," said Carmen. "He's always curious about what other people are thinking about Tiawanaku. He's not very 'open,' but always curious."

"I'm afraid I may have some small problems with him," I said, both Alex and I heaping our plates full of gooey, creamy pasta. We had hardly eaten a thing, for what, fifteen hours?

"I have problems with him too, but he's still fun," said Carmen, "He's not a bad guy, really– just a little 'closed'."

Ponce Sanginés was a great scholar in his own limited way and one of his earlier books, *Tunupa Y Ekako* (1969) on Ekekos, the hunchbacked dwarfs who were said to inhabit the ruins at Tiawanaku, had been very helpful to me in drawing lines between Bolivian crippled dwarfs and their equivalents in ancient Hindu, Greek and Egyptian mythology where they are also linked to mines and metals. What I had been able to do was link up the Greek Kabeiroi, the Egyptian Pataikoi, the Hindu Yaksas and the Bolivian Ekekos.* Essentially what we were talking about was Snow White's seven (miner) dwarfs … which came right out of Germanic/Teutonic folklore. Or the Celtic Leprechauns.

"Well, it's nice to be back here with you all," I said, sampling a little wine, everything calm inside me, Dette and all the others purring for a change instead of growling. I was where I should be, doing what I was supposed to be doing, all stasis and fulfilment, but somehow, on the edges of all this calm, a lot of, if not 'static,' then a sense of anticipation. Something "big" was about to happen, looming on the horizon, still invisible, but about to make its appearance.

First, though, we needed to collapse a while, and after our late lunch/early dinner, Alex and I went into our little place and got under the feather comforters and were instantly out.

"Get up when you want, the house is yours. It's going to take a couple of days until you get back on any kind of normal schedule after a trip like the one you've just gone through. And it takes a few days to get used to the altitude," Carmen had said as she had closed the door on us and it had the effect of a goodnight prayer on both of us, the waving of The Good Fairy's wand …

We were totally, totally out. It was like death, really. The thin air, the quiet house, the thick walls, whatever traffic there might have been in the far distance.

I was dreaming that I was in some sort of riverine Underworld, lost on dead rivers under heavy, overhanging trees, gloomy, shadowy, tenebrous, in Tartarus, under Hades trying to find my way back to the sun … when I suddenly woke up and looked at the little travel clock with the luminous dial that I had put on the bedside table next to me before going to sleep.

It was three a.m.

I went to the washroom and intended going back to bed, but my interior world was all in a snarling, snapping vicious state of unrest. I was tired of it. Possession. Psychotic snarls that weren't there … and then the

---

* More recently for the Old World material on dwarfs I have relied heavily on Veronique Dasen's *Dwarfs in Ancient Egypt and Greece*, Oxford: The Clarendon Press, 1993.

voice of Dette, her 'presence' slowly surrounding me as I pulled on my wool poncho and followed where she (and the others) wanted me to go, afraid of disturbing the household, tripping some kind of night-alarm, arousing some hidden dog, waking Mariano and Carmen or Carmen's mother, although I knew their bedrooms were way on the other side of the house in another wing, so I probably couldn't have even roused them if I'd wanted to. Walking down cold stone steps with bare feet, then over rough woven mats, the rich oriental rug in the living room:

"Relax ... tonight is one of those nights of illumination, a night to push back the Great Dark a little, the great curtain of *oscuridão*, darkness ... be patient with us as we have been patient with you, our little brother who slowly grows in the arts of light and become more and more one with *us* ..."

Going into Mariano's study where his collection of Pre-Columbian ceramics was, little glass-covered display cases filling the walls, on the far wall a huge collection of books on the Pre-Columbian and other ancient cultures.

I turned on the lights, lit up all the cabinets, found myself being pulled over to a cabinet with a Mochica pot it in, an old familiar pot, the Mochica fanged-god strangling the sea-serpent man.

The Mochica Indians whose culture was centred on the northern Peruvian coast, had suddenly begun some time around 150 B.C.

They had a very strange style in the drawings on their pots. "Strange" precisely because it wasn't strange, but oddly familiar, like ...

Mochica Pot of Fanged-God Strangling the Sea-Serpent Man

Dette-Teresita suddenly very strongly *there* in the room, as if she were somehow (how can I describe the sensation) … somehow … wound around myself … as if my soul were the tree in the garden of Eden, the tree in the Land of the Sun-King, and she were the serpent-dragon wound around it, guarding the apples of life, not growling now but hissing, "Think, remember, you have the answer inside you, who kills the sea-serpent man?"

Who kills the sea-serpent man?

I knew, of course I knew, but my memory wasn't what it used to be. I would forget the names of my own colleagues at the university, run into them in the hall and not remember their name until five minutes later when I was in my office, switching on my computer or starting to grade papers …

Who kills the sea-serpent man?

And then suddenly it was there: Herakles.

Hercules in Latin, Herakles in the original Greek.

Only what connection could there possibly be between Herakles and the Mochica Fanged-God?

I looked hard at the figure. It was wearing some sort of hat made out of a cat.

Herakles always wore a lion-skin. That was one of his major feats – the killing of the Nemean Lion. Which meant that the sun (Herakles as sun-god) had passed through the constellation of Leo the Lion.

On some Greek pots, in fact, Herakles wore the lion's head in such a way that it looked like he was emerging out of the lion's mouth:

Could it be that the Fanged-God's cat-hat on the Mochica pot was the Mochica equivalent of Herakles lion-skin hat in Greek art?

All I wanted to do was sleep, if need be stretch out on the leather couch here in Mariano's workroom and cover myself with the thick wool blanket that was stretched out all over it as a kind of slip-cover. I felt half-dissolved, exhausted, my whole body heavy, every joint aching. It was as if I had landed on Jupiter and the force of gravity had tripled, quadrupled ...

Only the hissing wouldn't stop, Dette-Teresita had no mercy. There were things that I had to do and discover.

"Look at the paws!" she hissed at me and I looked carefully at the paws of the cat on the cat hat and slowly saw them as letters somehow shaped into the fore and hindlegs of the cat (lion): N and L. Our letters. Only 'our' alphabet was essentially Phoenician. They were a Phoenician N and L. Which would mean you wouldn't write them from left to right, but from right to left, essentially 'backwards' in our terms. And they would be like Hebrew, consonant-words with 'implied' vowels.

Only what did LN mean?

All my years of Hebrew, my insane obsessiveness with semitic (and Proto-Indo-Mediterranean roots), my study at home lined with dictionaries, studies of comparative linguistics – *Dravidian Origins and the West. A Dravidian Etymological Dictionary. Semitic Roots* ... Tomback's *Comparative Semitic Lexicon of the Phoenician and Punic Languages*. Suddenly it was there at the centre of the blackboard of my mind. LN meant 'to complain,' 'murmur' ... GROWL ...

Clever, very clever on the artist's part, to have turned the claws of Herakles' lion-hat into a word that meant *growl*. An artist who obviously knew Phoenician and was very much inside of Greek myth. What did it mean, that the Mochicas were transplanted Phoenicians?

Mochica culture begins around 150 B.C. What major event took place around that time? Of course! In 146 B.C. the Romans had finally destroyed Carthage just outside of what is present-day Tunis. One of the most terrifying and dramatic events of ancient history.

There had been a war going on between Carthage and Rome for decades and finally the Romans and Carthaginians had come to a kind of truce. Carthage was to disarm, leave herself totally defenceless; and in exchange for this disarming, Rome was to respect Carthage's rights. Only after Carthage had disarmed, there was a debate in the Roman senate and some senators said that the only way that there was going to be any real peace was to destroy Carthage altogether. So the Romans came at night and made a surprise attack, coming through the Carthaginian fields, outside her walls, laying siege, the Carthaginians fighting back, melting down their statues, trying to manufacture arms, but the Romans finally getting inside and burning everything down, levelling the whole town and sowing the site with salt so that nothing would ever grow there.

It wasn't really that unexpected, though. The Romans had already taken over Gadés, the site of present-day Cadíz, on the Atlantic side of the Strait of Gilbraltar – *which had been the site of the most important Herakles temple in the ancient world.*

I already knew that the Phoenicians had been in the New World as far back as 1,000 B.C.– at the time of Solomon … eight hundred and fifty four years earlier!

I suddenly remembered reading in my favourite Greek-Sicilian historian, Diodorus Siculus (Diodorus the Sicilian), all about the fact that Phoenicians had discovered an immense 'island' in the West (South America, of course!) and the fact that the Tyrians (the people of Tyre) had wanted to establish a colony there but the Carthaginians had blocked the idea of such a colony because they wanted to keep it as an open option should the need ever arise for them to flee Carthage.

And when the Romans had attacked Carthage, that was the time, wasn't it?

Had some Carthaginians escaped the siege, or had some of them anticipated what was coming and fled to South America? Or had the Herakles priests in Gadés/Cadíz, once the siege had got underway, begun to see the writing on the wall? I'd read somewhere (Diodorus?) that the Romans had maintained the temple of Herakles in Cadíz more or less as it had been under Phoenician rule. Did the Phoenician priests there see a Roman axe coming down on their necks and flee to Peru? Was there some sort of alliance between some ship captains from Carthage who had escaped the Romans and the Herakles priests in Cadíz? The Romans had also conquered Corinth in Greece in 146 B.C., and there was an uncanny resemblance between Mochica pottery and Corinthian (especially Proto-Corinthian) ware. Were the potters originally Corinthian? I didn't know of any pottery either in Carthage or Spain that came close in quality to Mochica-ware.

Mariano must have had three hundred Mochica pots in his collection. Plus pieces from Nazca on the southern Peruvian coast, Chancay (just above Lima), a couple of Mixtec pieces from Mexico … but mainly he'd concentrated on the Mochicas. There was one pot that showed the Fanged God/Herakles, with just the outline of his lion-hat drawn in, fighting a crab:

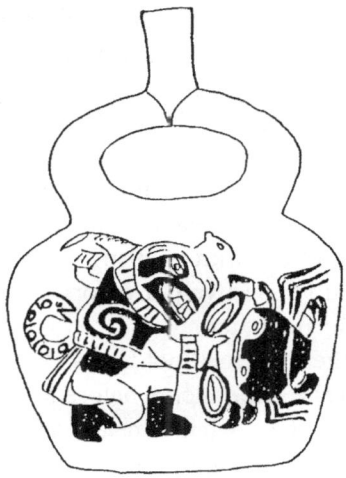

One of the major events in Herakles myths is when Herakles is battling the Lernaean Hydra and Hera sends a giant crab to attack him. Herakles kills the crab and it ascends into the heavens to become the constellation Cancer. That little incident was one of the clues that led me to see all the Herakles myths as zodiac stories. One of the creatures that Herakles battles with becomes a constellation; by extrapolation didn't that mean that all the incidents were involved with constellations, that *all* the Herakles stories were one vast zodiac myth? There was another pot in Mariano's collection that showed someone tied to a stake, being eaten by vultures:

Prometheus Bound

One of the stories is about Herakles liberating Prometheus who has been tied to a stake and vultures come and eat his liver, only every morning he is restored to wholeness again – an obvious sun symbol, like the Egyptian sun-god going into the Underworld at night and battling all sorts of monsters. Prometheus is the Morning Star. Herakles is the sun. There was a kind of poetic redundancy in having the sun liberate the Morning Star because the ancients had seen that the Morning Star disappears at the time of the winter solstice when the days begin to get longer again and the sun figuratively is 'reborn' – so that they equated the reborn sun and the Morning Star.

Mariano had another Mochica pot that showed a child with a snake in each hand. I'd seen the same theme before on Mochica pots, but now for the first time I understand what it meant. When Herakles is born the goddess Hera sends snakes to kill him in his crib. So here was a Mochica pot depicting Herakles killing the snakes:

Herakles Killing the Snakes that Hera Has Sent to Kill Him

There was one pot that especially attracted my attention, unlike any other pot I had ever seen in my life. No scenes were portrayed on it. No myths. It was starkly and totally geometric, but a geometry that said absolutely nothing to me:

I sat there staring at it. It was four a.m. on the pendulum clock on the wall. Only I wasn't tired now. My mind was pure clarity. It was like a thousand foot pool of chemically pure water that looked one foot deep. I felt like an Aztec crystal skull, Dette hissing inside me: "This is your moment of maximum clarity, the moment when you can see all things, understand Reality to its crystal core. Concentrate!"

The voices of long-dead Desaná shamans blew like soft winds through my mind: "The door of the horizon opens …"

When you take the sacred drug, *the door of the horizon opens!*

The Greek *delta*, Hebrew *daleth*. Δ

If one of the designs on the pot was a letter, then they must all be letters. The pot itself must be a word. The loop on top reminded me of early pro-Canaanite scripts:

Later Hebrew (the Mesha Stele) scripts:

Or (reversed) an Arabic L:

Obviously I was dealing with an 'L' here. I had two letters – D and L.

And the main outline of the figure, the steps? There was only one alphabet that I could remember that had a step as a letter – Old Thaumudic. The alphabet of the Philistines, a people who had lived on the Levantine coast *just below the Phoenicians!* Was it so crazy to imagine that the Phoenicians had 'borrowed' a letter from the Philistines to serve their symbolic needs?

= G

G-D-L. ... my head suddenly flooding with possible words that I created by adding variant vowels – GADOL – GEDDEL ... something 'great,' 'large,' 'exalted' ... or the sense of rebirth.

Of course! What was the whole centre of this ancient world? Rebirth at the time of the winter solstice. Suddenly remembering a drawing in Posnansky's monumental work on Tiawanaku, a drawing of the central 'pyramid' at Tiawanaku – the so-called Akapana:

Another 'revelation' flashed through me. The Akapana was a representation of half a year wasn't it? The time between the Autumnal Equinox and the Winter Solstice. And if you halved the shape of the Akapana, you came up with the basic shape of the Phoenician-Mochica word-pot:

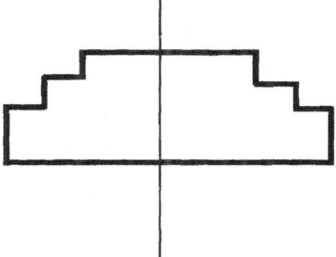

So the pot itself was representation of that final climactic moment of the year when the Faithful, the Blessed, the Gods themselves would take the sacred drug, their divine Communion, and renew their godlikeness ...

And when Herakles aged ...

I looked at yet another Herakles pot that had the L and N disguised as the front and rear paws of his lion hat, looked at the body of the figure itself – and there it was, the same stepped-pyramid motif:

The aged Herakles represented the sun at the end of the year, his face, in my mind, merging with Tata Wari, the Old Fire God, and I lay back, my mind slowly filled with the ruins at Tiawanaku themselves, the ruins and all the vast plains that surrounded them, the shortest day of the year, Jesus, the Sun-God is interred and put in his tomb, and the plains begin to fill with the faithful, all carrying their thorn-apple cacti or some sort of trumpet flowers or mushrooms, the drugs themselves for the most part interchangeable, the divine mind-activation drug clothed in a myriad of forms, the sun dead, among The Dead, in Hell ... and then the year turning, the sun resurrecting, the fire-god/sun-god himself, call him Helios or Con, Viracocha, Ra, Votan, The Christ, it made no difference ... walking up to the top of the Akapana, the centre of the centre, the Holy of Holies, himself taking the divine drug as thousands of The Faithful followed his example and took their drugs and died and were resurrected and the whole plain became a snarling mass of triumphant resurrection.

I knew they had *all* been there in the past. The Huichols in Northern Mexico took their Peyote and were transported to the Land of Wiracuta which was the Land of Viracocha (Tiawanaku), the Hopi and Zuñi had emerged from the Underworld and gone to the Home of the Gods, Itiwanna [Tiawanaku] the Place in the Middle, Tawakihu, Sun, his House ...

The Holy Spirit *did* enter them and they all became Lions of Judah. That was what the fangs on the Fanged God, Herakles, was all about, wasn't it, an essential, spiritual transformation into shamanhood, the place where I had come to.

It was all greatness (*gadol*) and rebirth (*geddel*), an ascent into Heaven.

The realisation of what I had discovered flooded through me. It was the first time that *anyone had seen a very specific Old World mythological system (in this case the Herakles myths) as the basis for the religion of an entire New World 'tribe' of people.*

The theory that the New World had been exclusively inhabited across the Bering Strait during the Ice Ages was finally demolished and a New Era had begun, and all the other linguistic and artistic and mythological pieces fell into place. The very fact that the centre of Herakles myth was this death and resurrection pivot-point tied together all the other myths about heroes (the sun) going to the Land of the Sun King/The Tin Lands where the magic apples of immortality were.

Only what about The Götterdämmerung, the Twilight of the Gods?

Sigfried, the Young Sun, came to Valhalla, the Home of the Gods ... but in Germanic myth the gods *did* die.

But how could they have died when they still surrounded me, filled the room, my head, my very being, as real as any pot, as real as the sofa I stretched out on, as real as the heavy woollen blanket I covered myself over with ... as real as sleep, as real as dreams ... death ... resurrection ...

"*Hugo! Estas bien, Hugo!* – Hugh, are you OK?"

I opened my eyes. Mariano was there standing over me. It was morning. Impossibly, intrusively bright.

"I'm fine," I said, sitting up, announcing: "All these Mochica pots show scenes from Phoenician-Greek Herakles mythology. There are Phoenician words on the pots," showing him the LGN and LN, taking down the GDL stepped-pyramid pot, "and this pot actually is a Phoenician word connected with rebirth ..."

"But do you know Phoenician?"

"Hebrew. It's – if not the same language, closer than dialect-differences in English in England, say the Midlands and Cockney in London. *Adon* in Hebrew, for example, is 'Lord.' *Adon Olam* is Lord of the world. *Adon* in Phoenician is *Adonis*, The Hebrew *Melech* (King) is *Melgart* ... very close ... Tiawanaku was the centre of ancient world religion and myth ... the Anaku of Sumerian myth ..."

"Remember Cieza de León," he answered, "when he first came to the ruins at Tiawanaku and was totally overwhelmed by them. They obviously were something 'key,' important, totally impressive. And there they were off the world cultural map, a totally unknown quantity ... you ought to have a lot of fun with Mario Montaña Aragón this afternoon ... the two of you see eye to eye, I guess ..."

"I owe a lot to his work," I said, "but even more," (lowering my voice as if the room were bugged and The Enemy was out to record every word I said) "I owe even more to my 'jaguars.'"

"Jaguars?"

"I'm living full-time on psychedelic drugs now," I said, dipping into my pyjama pocket and fishing out a few Datura seeds.

"Why not?" said Mariano, "Everyone else around here does ... it's the core of most indigenous religions ..." then getting 'official,' glancing down at his watch, "well, I'd better get going. I always have a quick breakfast at the office. Things get a little overwhelming at this time of the year. I'll see you tonight and we can talk more."

And he left, and I lay back down. In a little while Carmen's mother came down and she and the maid started breakfast. I went back to our room and stretched out in my bed just a few moments longer, Carmen finally knocking on my door.

"Hugo, it's time for breakfast!"

"OK, pal, I'll be right out."

Alex waking up. One thing she liked to do was to sleep late, but when she smelled the coffee and milk and *dulce de leche* (evaporated sweetened milk), she revived and got up. "Brother, am I hungry."

And we both went out, returned to The World again, sat down and had breakfast.

That afternoon I met Mario Montaño Aragón at one of the big cafés in downtown La Paz. Alex came along. And we all had *coca*-leaf tea. I remember eating an eclair, Alex a big gooey piece of chocolate cake. Everyone in Bolivia chewed *coca* leaves from the time they were kids. It wasn't so much a drug as Medicine against the terrible altitude and cold. For me at this point it was merely like a not particularly strong cup of coffee.

Mario was skinny and emaciated as usual.

He was a minor government functionary by day and a top-rate scholar by night, not part of scholarly officialdom like Ponce Sanginés, but a man of great insights and erudition.

"I hear you have a book you want me to publish!" I said as we sat down, "something revolutionary."

"You know the links," he said, heavily dosing his *coca*-tea with sugar, "the links between Sumerian and the Bantu languages of Africa … but I've just finished a book linking up Turkish and Aymara."

Aymara was the principal language spoken in the Bolivian *altiplano*. The Aymara Indians were a tall, powerful race who tended to dominate everything they touched.

"*Turkish and Aymara?*"

He reached into a worn briefcase and pulled out an enormous manuscript. I glanced through it and was instantly 'converted.'

Of course it made all the sense in the world.

I already knew that Quechua, the other main 'Indian' language in the Andes was linked to Sanskrit and Sumerian. I knew, in turn, that Sumerian was linked to the Indus Valley, that Elamite, the language of Elam, right next to the Persian Gulf, was linked to the Dravidian languages of India and that you could trace the movement of the Sumerians out of the Persian Gulf into Africa by showing the links between Sumerian and the African Bantu languages … by the same token you could see (in a book like *Dravidian Origins and the West*) the Dravidian links to any number of Black African languages. The broad swath of movement was clear. Movement out of what is today Turkey into what is today Iraq, movement out of what is today Pakistan, down the African coast, and up the west side of Africa and then across to the New World. Now Mario Montaño Aragón had simply shown a direct link between Turkey (Asia Minor/Anatolia) and the Bolivian *altiplano*. Ancient Turks, ancient Indians from India, ancient Sumerians, Phoenicians, all the tribes of the Middle East and India had been in ancient Tiawanaku when it still was the functional centre of world myth.

I was glancing at his book thinking that, yes, maybe I could publish it under my Ghost Dance Press name, when suddenly 'the madness' descended on me, a kind of epileptic fit that wasn't a fit at all, but a spiritual whirl and flurry that always preceded a revelation. Revelations never came easily but always had violent births.

"Are you OK?" asked Mario.

'*Tom*,' I answered, with a long 'o' as in 'tome.'

"*Tov?*" he asked, the Hebrew for good.

"*Tom*," I repeated, and then "*Tamima, Temima*," Hebrew, Syriac, Aramaic, images tumbling through my head, reaching out and grabbing a napkin and taking a pen out of the breast pocket of my tweed jacket, starting to draw:

Mario's face slowly brightening as I covered the napkins with what were obviously variations of the basic G-D-L design I had discovered on the Mochica letterpot.

"Yes, yes … I recognise the designs … Hacilar … Turkey … 6,000 B.C."

Only I was still in a whirlwind, a vortex of ancient associations.

"K … k … ka …" Hebrew, Aramaic, Arabic … "like."

Only like what? Suddenly plunged into a moment of total darkness like I was having a stroke, a heart attack. Frozen. Dead. My head back, the jaguars in my mind tearing my neck open, my heart out, *Agnus Dei*, the Lamb of God, *Agnus* as in *Agni*, the Hindu fire god.

Starting to draw again as I slowly 'softened' and re-emerged into the light, a waiter coming over, concerned, "*Llamo un medico?*/Should I call a doctor?"

"*No, estoy bien de nuevo.* No, I'm OK again."

"I'm afraid I don't recognise these ... although they're the same general signs, I suppose," said Mario.

Language, my own language, suddenly coming back into me with a whoosh.

"They're designs from Anasazi pots in New Mexico. The same as designs from prehistoric Colombia." And I quickly drew a design from a plate from Boyacá:

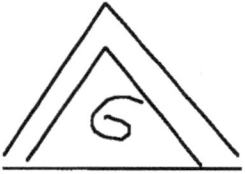

"And they link up with the Dimeni Culture in Greece," I explained, "the same step motifs, the triangular delta-daleth door, the spiral of rebirth ..."

"Amazing," said Mario, "so it's all in the pots too, isn't it? I don't work all that much in iconography and scripts, mainly in linguistics ... but I can see it... the Dimeni Culture, goes back to ... ?"

"Five thousand B.C."

"Before Greece was inhabited by the Greeks, while the Proto-Indo-Mediterranean Mother Goddess peoples still inhabited the whole of Asia Minor and the Mediterranean, up into the Balkans ... out into the New World."

I couldn't help myself. I got up and went over to him and gave him a strong *abrazo*.

"Dad!" complained Alexandra, "Everyone's looking at you."

My eyes filled with tears.

"*Estamos entre amigos* – we are among friends," I told her, "they're just curious, not censorious. And there is a difference."

An Anasazi Pot From New Mexico (left) and an Analagous Design on a Dish from Boyacá, Colombia

A Pot from the Dimini Culture in Mainland Greece

The Same Design from Hacilar, Turkey

The Same Design on a Pot From Tiawanaku

I had suddenly made another link, bringing archaeology back to the origins of the Anasazi back from New Mexico, to Casa Grande in Mexico, to Colombia, back to the peoples who inhabited mainland Greece in Neolithic Times.

Mario was exaltant. It seemed that everything I had discovered merely confirmed his own ideas about ancient links between the Middle East-Turkey and the Andes.

He went on for quite a while on his own observations. I ate another eclair, Alexandra had another piece of cake. I found Mario's observations totally fascinating.

Alexandra, of course, was only twelve. It wasn't just a question of an incomplete knowledge of Spanish, but the specialised vocabulary that Mario was using:

"You know how in Hebrew you used the word MINHA for vegetable offerings in the Temple in Jerusalem in ancient times. Well, move back to the Andes ... take the word MINKCAYKUNI in Quechua, meaning 'to ask favours from the saints.' Of course we're separated from the Pre-Columbian by five hundred years, and I'm not saying the Quechua people are Jews ... but there are thousands and thousands of these sorts of Semitic-Quechua-Aymara links. MINA – to offer something up to God. MINCAKUNI – to ask for God's favour. Even the pronunciation shows the link, the special guttural 'ka' – min-c-ka ..."

After about an hour of Mario's discoursing on linguistics, Alex tugged at the sleeve of my jacket.

"How about walking around a little?"

"OK," I said, turning to Mario, "*Ella esta un poco ... como puedo decir* ... she's a little ... how can I put it ..."

"*Aburrida*/Bored!" laughed Mario. "No problem. I was glad to have as much time with you as I've had. It's nice to have an ally in the US."

We all got up. More embraces.

I felt a tremendous sense of loss, exaggerated, perhaps, but I had a feeling that I would never see him again. Maybe it was my sacred drugs, but I had begun to live in a sense of *All Time* now. It wasn't an occasional sense of the true dimensions of Time and Space, but a continuous awareness of the ticking of the Big Clock in the Sky ... tick, tick, tick, tick ... *wir haben nur einmal, einmal und nichts mehr, gewesen zu sein* ... we only have once, once and not more, to be ... although 'to be' doesn't really adequately translate Rilke's German – *gewesen zu sein*. The German has almost a studied redundancy, something like to-be to-be ... once to-be to-be ...

"*Hasta Luego!*" he said as we went out the door and he sat down again, poured a little more water over the little bag of coca leaves in his cup, "Until later ..."

But I 'knew,' didn't I, deep inside me, that *luego*/later would become *nunca*/never.

We walked around downtown for a while, I bought a shoulder bag made out of beautifully tanned, heavy leather with a piece of old weaving decorating the flap. Maybe fifty years old. Filled with rows of the old, familiar sun symbol:

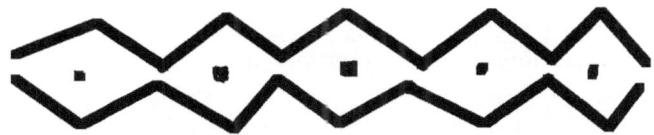

I bought Alexandra a pair of silver earrings and necklace. My OAS grant didn't pay a lot but Dette would send me a *mensualidad*/allowance every month, and prices, in this most forgotten of historical backwaters, were incredibly low.

It was the ultimate irony, wasn't it, that the Home of the Gods had become a miserable, castoff piece of the Third World at its most third-worldliness.

There was the smell of human shit everywhere. Lots of homeless Indians. And restaurants wouldn't let them in to use the toilets. So what else could they do? Urine and faeces everywhere, the air filled with a feeling of despair. These were the great races of the holy ancients and now they were totally marginalised and cast out into homeless poverty.

"Let's go back to Carmen's and Mariano's," Alexandra said after a little while, and we took a cab to the bottom of the hill where the Baptistas lived, got out, had to pass through the police-guard into that area, show our passports, the whole schmear.

Once they got to know us, OK, but what were we supposed to be, potential terrorists ... ? It was like France before the French Revolution, wasn't it? The nobles in their castles, the poor in the streets ...

That evening, after what they called *Te*/Tea, but what was a nice light dinner of salami and cheese, bread, coffee, jellies and cakes (the main meal being at noon, just the reverse of practices in the US, but exactly along the same lines as the Mediterranean), Carmen invited me up to the master bedroom and started showing me her latest paintings. Which I really wasn't that crazy about. Kind of like painted cartoons. I remember one of Leonardo da Vinci in bed with Mona Lisa, the caption something like "I imagine you'd have something to smile about too!"

"I'm totally market-oriented these days," she confessed, "that's what people want, that's what people get. I'm not picky and choosy and idealistic the way I used to be."

I loved the bedroom. High ceiling. Lots of room. The bed was a double kingsize. Specially made. The house really was the Palace of San Souci – without sorrow.

Only then something started gnawing at me inside again. Like a rat chewing on the walls of my soul. Or squirrels in the attic, rats in the basement.

Carmen was going on about some guy in New York who was collecting her paintings.

"He's got about twenty now, is talking about 'launching' me into the New York market. You know how it is once you catch on. Who would have ever thought that someone pouring paint all over canvases, splattering and smearing, like Jackson Pollock, would ever have caught on. Or all of Warhol's silly silk screens of Marilyn Monroe. But that's what happens ... you just never know ..."

She was a beautiful woman, creamy skin, filled out a little now in middle age.

Just what I liked. I never liked women who were all bone, anorexic, bulimic, negating their own flesh. She must have dyed her hair black – it was just all too perfect. And the way she was dressed, all in roughish, soft blue cotton, wearing black tights and alpargates.

I loved to be with her, loved to listen to her, but The Thing inside me wouldn't let go. I was the cobra and it was the mongoose, and it wouldn't get shaken loose; no matter what yogic exercises I tried, the gnawing continued, rolling, tumbling waves of jaguar growls growing inside me.

Finally it got so bad that she noticed and stopped.

"Are you all right, Hugo?"

"I'm 'possessed,'" I confessed, "the drugs I've been taking for the last twenty years. They give me certain 'powers,' but like everything else, you pay the price. There's something else I'm supposed to 'discover' tonight. Something in this house ... down in Mariano's study ..."

"What do you mean?" asked Carmen, all curious now. "How do you know?"

"I'm being directed from inside. They direct me. It's something beyond words."

"Can I come along?" she said.

"As far as I know ..."

I got up and started down the stairs, past the portrait of Mariano's grandfather as president of Bolivia. All sorts of little pots and pictures hung on the walls. One Mimbres pot, wasn't it, that was structurally almost identical with pots from Susa in Elam, on the edge of ancient Mesopotamia.

Mimbres Pots from American Southwest

Pots from Susa

My head was like a museum of world pottery, a library of world myth, comparative linguistics, rows and rows of dictionaries, monographs like David McAlpin's *Proto-Elamo-Dravidian: The Evidence and Its Implications* (*Transactions of the American Philosophical Society*, Vol.71, Part 3, 1981) that linked Susa (Elam) with the Dravidian languages of India ... just seeing the Mimbres pot setting a whole chain of associations tumbling through my head ... the Elamite word *anak* meaning "to shine" ... what better meaning could there be for TIAWANAKU, the home of the Sun-King?

Down to Mariano's study.

He wasn't there, had had to go back to the office for a while, smiling as he left: "Even the Minister of Education has to do his homework!"

Ha, ha, ha, ha ...

The 'forces' inside me very specific. I was being directed to a case of pre-Columbian pots on the far wall. There was a rather crudely typed label on one of the shelves – Condorhuasi Culture, Argentina.

A culture I knew very little about.

I had spent one year in Buenos Aires studying Latin American culture at the University there, had given a lecture at the University of the Chaco, had been to La Plata ... but never up into the Argentinian Andes where, I remembered, the Condorhuasi Culture had been located.

I looked carefully at the head of the figure:

Head of Figure from the Condorhuasi Culture in Argentina

There was something else I was supposed to remember. Something else in this room that was screaming at me. Whenever I was 'on track' the jaguar-growls inside me would be almost harmonious, in chorus, but when I strayed to the left or right, up or down, it would be pure cacophony.

I was being directed to a volume in Mariano's collection of books on ancient art.

I totally negated my own Will and let myself be guided – *not my will but thine be done*. Pure passivity. And my hand reached up and pulled down a volume on ancient Turkish pottery. Again Hacilart, Turkey, at the 6,000 B.C. level.

"What are you looking for, Hugo?" whispered Carmen as if she could hear the choir of jaguar voices purring inside me.

"I don't know," I answered as my hand automatically started flipping through the pages and stopped when I had got to a picture of the head of a figure that almost exactly matched up with the Condorhuasi head.

Hacilart, Turkey

Another link ... and my mind was filled with streams of rafts and ancient high-prowed almost Viking-looking boats, some of wood, some of reeds, travelling around Africa, travelling through the Mediterranean, through the Strait of Gibraltar, across the Pacific, island hopping.

And then a series of sudden visions lightninged through my mind, like a series of punches on the back of my neck, like buckets of cold water being poured all over me. An image of a Proto-Chavín bone carving from Northern Peru. Chavin, the Home of Yama, the Lord of the Underworld:

Then the image of a Shang Dynasty pot dating from around 1,500 B.C.:

Then the sudden, searing image of a puma shaman-master from Tiawanaku itself with the head of the shaman neophyte between its forepaws:

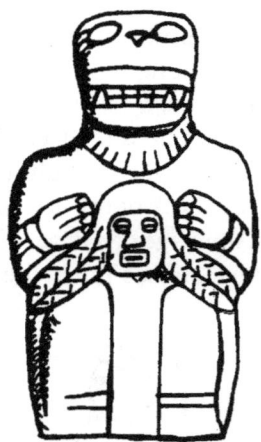

Of course I understood what the figure of the man engulfed by the feline (tiger-jaguar-puma) meant. It was the great Feline Spirit from the Real World opened up by the sacred hallucinogens. It was *me* surrounded by, controlled by my jaguars. I was no longer a free agent but merely an instrument of the Spirits bringing forth their millennial message to the material (modern) world.

Another image suddenly smashed into front stage centre in my mind, the image of a hedgehog head from Puerto Hormiga on the Columbian coast, 3,000 B.C. Followed immediately by a Greek Hedgehog Burial Urn from a much later timelayer – 800 B.C.

Puerto Hormiga 3,000 B.C.

Greece 800 B.C.

"Are you OK, Hugo … ?"

I could hear Carmen's voice, as if it were coming through a thick brick wall. She was outside the theatre and I was inside, an old dead theatre … looking up at the giant screen, totally alone, one image after another slicing across my eyes. There was an outline of a Frog Goddess from a Bohemian dish on the 6,000 B.C. level, almost exactly the same as a Frog Goddess on a Marajoara pot from Brazil.

Czech Frog Goddess

Frog Goddess From Brazil

I couldn't envision a direct line between the Czech Republic and Brazil, but the same peoples who had inhabited Bohemia in 6,000 B.C. had made it across the Atlantic, if not at the 6,000 B.C. level, certainly by 3,000 B.C. The 'lazy,' horizontal S on the top of a Marajoara pot from Brazil …

… matched up exactly with the same S on the pubic triangle of a Great Goddess figure from Neolithic Trace, an area now divided between Greece and Turkey:

The speed and rapidity and startling vividness of the images was overwhelming. Images I had stored in my mind for years, lying like seeds waiting for the fertilising rain of this moment. The strange knobby figures from ancient Trinidad suddenly linked up with the Greek Prodromo Culture:

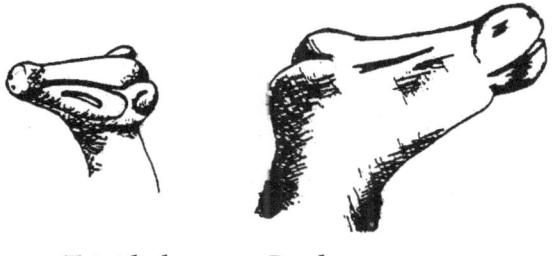

Trinidad   *Prodromo*

The 'official version' of the origins of the peoples who had inhabited the Caribbean, the Atacama Desert, the Andes, Mexico and the American Southwest had nothing to do with the reality of the neolithic migrations out of Europe/The Middle East to the Americas, great masses of peoples who saw the universe as a giant mother-goddess womb, the Great Mother as frog-, or bear-, or monkey-goddess, all the varieties of her divine epiphanies in the world always essentially the same, whether she came from northwestern Venezuela …

... or the south Balkans at the 6,000 B.C. level:

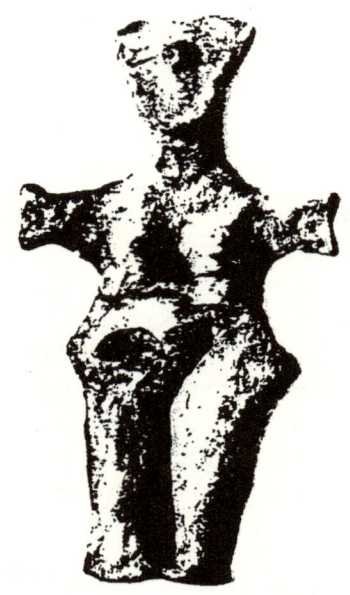

Then the Sun-God peoples had followed the Earth-Goddess peoples to the New World, and somewhere along the line the sacred drugs had been discovered and men had become gods. Or were they already some special extra-terrestrial race who had landed in Israel (and the Andes) with messages and agendas from outer (inner) space ... ?

Slowly the mad image-show inside my head subsided and I came back into my body, into the room, Carmen's arms around me, my arms around her, like a child hanging desperately on to its mother in the midst of a wild nightmare.

"Are you OK, Hugo?" she asked solicitously. "Do you want me to take you to a hospital?"

"Not really," I said, still holding on to her as Alex (who had been in our room watching old BBC programmes, for some reason especially fascinated by *UpstairsDownstairs*) came into the room, amused at seeing us so intimately intertwined.

"Well, excuse me, you two!"

Carmen disentangled herself and moved back on the couch.

"Your father was having some sort of 'attack.'"

"Not an 'attack,'" I corrected her, "a series of visions ..."

"About what?" asked Alex.

"Connections between New and Old World cultures. It was like a high-voltage speeded-up slide show," I explained.

"Neat-O!" she said, actually envious, her whole life as always centred on the eye, line, form, texture. More than anyone else I had ever known, she was a *born artist!*

"Let me make you some herbal tea," said Carmen and we went back into the dining room, had some tea and some chocolate-chip oatmeal cookies that Carmen brought out in a big cookie jar of a pig standing on its hind legs, that reminded me of the Neolithic pig goddesses – another form/manifestation of the Great Goddess.

After we finished Carmen was still worried about me.

"I have a friend, Hugo, a general practitioner. I'm certain that if I asked him to, he would come over and take a look at you."

"No, really, it's not that unusual. When you become a shaman you're mainly in the 'real' world – not *this* world," touching the table, the plates, my own hands and arms, "but the 'real' world ..."

The world of the so-called 'saints', the world of incarnations and transfigurations and assumptions into heavens, angels and devils, all very real for me now, even the dining room we were sitting in filled with half-visible 'presences' that threatened to step through the veil of Spirit into Flesh at any moment.

"I worry about you, my friend," said Carmen ... as Mariano came in with a big, heavy briefcase talking about budgets and social inequalities.

He joined us for tea and cookies, finally seemed to come back into the room himself as if he'd been transported into his own faerie realms and had his own difficulties coming into the Here and Now.

"So what's been going on around here?"

"Hugo has been having visions," Carmen explained.

"I've eaten my last thorn-apple," said Alex, smiling, "believe me."

"My mind started putting together data that I had been archiving in my mind," I tried to explain, "all kinds of iconographic links between, say, China and Chavín, Neolithic Greece and Turkey and the Atacama Desert, the Argentinian Andes, Trinidad, Northern Brazil ... you know, the island of Marajo in the mouth of the Amazon ... and eventually up into Northern Mexico. Two sacred areas, really, the Tropic of Capricorn and the Tropic of Cancer. It's not by accident that Tenochitlan, the Aztec capital, Teotehuacan, the La Venta culture, Chichen Itzá in Mexico are all on and around the Tropic of Cancer, the 'other' House of the Sun in the Northern Hemisphere."

"Hold on a second," said Mariano, getting up and going into his study, bringing back a book called *Argentina Indigena* by Dick Edgar Ibarra Grasso, an author I already knew, the professor who had written a book that had been a key source for me, *La Escritura Indigena Andina*, where, for the first time, I had seen the Indus Valley alphabet that had been in use in the Andes at the time of the Conquest. He thumbed through the book for a moment and opened it up to a series of diagrams that showed the similarities of pottery styles and motifs in South America and Northern Mexico/the American Southwest. During all periods, from the very earliest on (the so-called "Basketmaker" Period) up to the time of the Spanish Conquest, the implication being, of course, that there had always been constant contact between the areas around the two Tropics, all through pre-history.

"You're amazing!" I told him, "you ought to have gone into archaeology."

"Who says I haven't !" he smiled.

"Oh, Hugo, I almost forgot. Maria del Carmen, my daughter, called up earlier and said that she and her husband are going past Tiawanaku on the day after tomorrow. She's doing an interview with some priest who's supposed to be some kind of saint or something and she wondered if you and Alexandra might like to get dropped off and picked up at Tiawanaku. You know, give you a few hours at the ruins themselves."

"It sounds good to me!" I said.

I hadn't seen Maria del Carmen for some years, still thought of her as a little girl, and here she was already married and a professional journalist.

The next afternoon Alex and I got to the home of Carlos Ponce Sanginés at about two in the afternoon. Another mansion in another fancy La Paz suburb. *Carlos Ponce Sanginés Eng.* on a little plaque on his front door. *Eng.* Engineer. And he never let you forget what he was.

"Well, it's good to finally meet you," he said, escorting us into his book-lined, cramped, very scholarly-looking study. "I've heard so much about you from Carmen and Mariano. We're very close. Have been for years and years. I hear that you're interested in Tiawnaku."

"Well, I've found out a few things," I said, just a trifle put off by the man's unconscious, unintentional officiousness, but deciding to open up anyhow, "things like the fact that Tiawanaku is already mentioned in Old World literature as far back as 3,000 B.C. as Anaku in the Sumerian epic *Gilgamesh*. Or the fact that in Luwian, the ancient language of Crete, *Tiwantinaku* means 'The Young Lord Brings Life,' *Tiwat* being the Luwian word for sun ... the sentence as a whole meaning that the young sun brings life back to the earth after the winter solstice ..."

"Three thousand B.C.?" he interrupted me, "I'm afraid your dates are way, way off. According to carbon dating and other scientific dating-methods, you're making Tiawanaku just a few thousand years older than it really is …"

"I see the Akapana as the source of worldwide winter-solstice symbolism and part of an actual word that uses steps as a letter to spell out Geddel – to sprout," I answered, ignoring the 'scientific dating-methods' remark altogether.

After three years of pre-Med and a year of Medicine, my father an M.D., my wife an M.D., all my life one thing more than anything else had been impressed on me, the genuinely theoretical nature of scientific theory. I was willing to give certainly as much credence to iconographic and stylistic similarities as I was to 'scientific dating methods.'

And I took out a little notebook that I always carried with me, tore out a page and wrote down:

Then spelled out Tiawanaku from the letters written on the ruins themselves:

◯ = TI   〰︎ = A   ⌐┐ = NAKU

"These are all ancient Middle Eastern and Indus Valley letters. Like I showed the *naku* symbol (⌐┐) to this great Kabbalistic scholar in New York, Menke Katz, and he immediately identified it as NAKASH, Hebrew for serpent, the Hebrew equivalent of the Sumerian NAKU …"

"It's true," said Ponce Sanginés with solemnity, just a touch of contempt in his voice, "it's true that from the Akapana on the day of the Winter Solstice, it's the only place in the ruins where you can see the sun rise up from behind Mount Illimani and set over Lake Titicaca … but your dates are totally off … totally unscientific …"

"Well, mightn't there be an altitude factor in the whole dating process?" I protested, "or maybe the sites you got samples from weren't the right sites. In a place like Tiawanaku – or Rome – that has been inhabited continuously over a period of thousands of years, you can find any date you want depending on the sample you choose. Maybe you haven't gone down far enough for your samples ..."

"Wrong, wrong, wrong, wrong," said Ponce Sanginés and the matter was closed. He was the voice of God, *ex cathedra*. No more discussion.

"OK," I said, getting up, picking up the piece of paper I'd written the two words on, "I guess that's that!"

"Let me have that paper!" he said impetuously, grabbed it out of my hand and stuck it in his pocket.

"So be it!" I said and we were escorted to the door, out into the bright, cold Bolivian sun.

"Remember me to Carmen and Mariano!"

And there we were alone in the empty street.

"What an arsehole!" said Alexandra.

"Well, I might as well get used to it," I answered as we started walking down to the main street that ran through La Paz and off of which everything branched and sub-branched, "I'm afraid that that's the kind of reaction I'm going to get from all officialdom. No-one's open. Everyone's dogmatic. They get inside their little towers of ignorance and defend themselves against all opposing ideas, anything new ..."

I was depressed, but Dette's voice inside of me told me not to be, what's the difference, *you have to see what you're up against, but you won't have much longer to worry about these things anyhow ... we will be together again forever ... soon, soon, soon ...*

All the rest of that afternoon, that night and the next morning I was in a kind of trance. Alex had been noticing that Mariano's schedule was full of irregularities and that there were huge unaccounted for time-spaces.

"I wonder what's going on," she said.

"He's fine," I told her, not really wanting to come to grips with anything but me and the sacred world around me whose sacredness was growing by the minute, like I was spiritually getting ready for a long voyage myself, as if I were going on a space-launch of some kind and moving into some sort of long countdown.

But, of course, Alex, in her own prescient way, had picked up an irregularity in Mariano's life that later erupted into a scandal that would totally shatter several people's lives. He had another woman on the side. For more than twelve years. Another woman. Another daughter. It was incredible that he had been able to pull off such a thing in a world like that of La Paz where the upper crust was so minuscule and everything so transparent and commented on.

But I wasn't interested. There was a whole other modus operandi taking over inside me. Balloons were filling, stores were being stowed in the hold of my spirit; Tiawanaku, just a few short kilometers away, was calling to me. I felt Illimani, the great Thunder-Mountain, home of Indra the Lightning- and Storm-God, hovering heavily over the whole of La Paz, as if I could reach out and almost touch it, the angelic and the demonic mixing together inside me …

"Are you OK?" Alex finally asked me as we found a taxi and started back to Mariano's and Carmen's.

"Optimum!" I said.

I didn't know what was coming, but whatever it was, I was spiritually more than ready for it.

The next morning Maria del Carmen and her husband, Ricardo, came by about ten. We were both ready, although Alex wasn't quite sure if she wanted to go or not.

"It's so cold," she complained. And the cloudy weather bothered her, the days, now toward the end of June, getting shorter and shorter, as if the whole universe were running down.

"It's like the whole world is dying," she said over breakfast, "like a little piece of me is being chipped away every day."

"I know what you mean," said Carmen's mother, pouring her second cup of thick, rich coffee, adding hot, bubbly cream, "In Münich in the old days I'd get terribly sad around and before Christmas … *Ich weiß nicht was soll es bedeuten daß ich so traurig bin* … that's an old poem in German …" translating into Spanish, "*No se lo que significa que yo soy tan triste* …"

"Good translation!" said Carmen, always very proud of her little old mother. Maybe it was a prestige item to have a German mother in Bolivia?!

"I remember in New York around Christmas, when I used to work on *Pulpsmith*," I put my two cents in, "five thirty and it would always be dark. Just me and the boss would be left in the offices. Harry Smith. He always named his mags after himself – first *The Smith*. Then *Pulpsmith* when he wanted to get more 'popular.' I'd usually spend most of the Christmas vacation with him every year for almost twenty years. And it's true, right around Christmas the offices would get 'ghostly,' almost as if everyone who had ever worked there wanted to come back, as if the roads to Hell/ The Underworld were opened up …"

"You're giving me the creeps," said Carmen, getting up and putting another sweater around her shoulders.

Mariano was already gone. What he'd probably do would be to go over and have breakfast with his other wife every morning. But no one could have guessed it; he did it all so deftly and effortlessly. It was the kind of compartmentalisation that I would have been completely incapable of.

Things were a little existentially 'heavy' for a while, but then, when Maria del Carmen came, things brightened up.

She was a bright penny of a woman. The bright little girl had grown into a brilliant woman, kind of hippyish, beatnikish, bohemian, all jeans and boots and rough cotton jackets, both of them the same, Ricardo bearded, of course.

They had a nice kind of newish jeep. It was what you needed in Bolivia. Once you got outside of La Paz it was all dirt roads. Hardly roads at all, just ribbons of potholed confusion winding through wilderness. Instant time-travel back to the prehistoric.

Which in a way was perfect – one way to prevent the destruction of the millennial cultures that still inhabited the *altiplano* almost untouched and unchanged by the disease of The Modern.

"OK, see you later!" I said to Carmen and gave her a hug and a kiss, kissed and hugged the mother, and Socorro, the almost invisible little Indian maid, with most of her teeth gone in front, a couple of molars left for grinding her food. You would have thought that Carmen and Mariano would have got her some false teeth, but, of course, it may have occurred to me, it never would have occurred to them. There was "us" and "them." We were to be served; they were to serve. The mentality of the *Conquista* still alive and well.

It was only supposed to be a day's outing but, somehow, I knew better, knew that I would never see them again – at least in this life. Other lives … ? I wasn't sure.

It was a long drive out of the city to Tiawanaku and just as rough as I had expected. There were a couple of times when we hit potholes that would have broken the axles of lesser vehicles.

"There's this old priest living out with the Indians, about an hour beyond Tiawanaku. He is said to be a miracle-worker, preaching a new gospel for a new age. The perfect subject for a feature article, and who knows where it can go from here. Can't you just imagine picking up a copy of *Paris Match* and there's the article in French, my byline and all … ?"

"Why not?" I answered.

It was true enough, the world out there was hungry for any kind of spiritual message to fill its spiritual emptiness.

I dipped into my pocket and hunted up a few Datura seeds, started chewing on them. Speaking of spiritual emptiness ...

"It's fun for me to get out and see a little of the real world," said Ricardo, "mainly all I do is take pictures of corpses, brides, bridegrooms and newborn infants, births, baptisms, First Communions, weddings, The Dead ... no one ever seems to want pictures of divorces ..."

Ha, ha, ha, ha ...

They seemed like a perfect couple, like two pairs of old shoes thrown into an old suitcase together.

It must have taken an hour to get to the ruins themselves and they let us off next to a kind of crude, improvised restaurant/refreshment stand close to the entrance.

"So, listen, we'll be back by about five, how's that?" said Maria del Carmen, "there'll be a little light left. And anyhow, Ricardo has wonderful night vision. They don't call him El Lobo [the Wolf] for nothing."

"So we'll meet you right here!" said Ricardo, pointing to the restaurant/refreshment stand.

And there we were, left by ourselves as the jeep bumped off down the road into still more remote No Man's Lands.

"I feel depressed," said Alex as we made our way into the ruins themselves.

"Me too," I admitted, walking past gigantic slabs of beautifully worked stone all tumbled and broken. Not just ruins but pillaged ruins, for centuries used as a stone quarry to build churches like the Catholic church at Copacabana, stone for railway bridges, stone for buildings in La Paz. It was as if the great pyramids in Egypt had been dismantled in order to build Cairo.

I couldn't help but cry, put my arm around Alex as I walked into the ruins and saw what Ponce Sanginés and his crew had done to add insult to injury, reassembling the stone, putting drains up where there was nothing to drain, assembling stones the way they had never been assembled before, in my own mind slowly the ruins becoming what they were, a steady hum inside me, choirs of eagles and jaguars filling my mind, looking at The City That Had Been, all covered with gold-plate, shining in the sacred sun, walking up to the top of the Akapana, Mount Illimani to my left, calling to me with its gigantic thunder-voice in the sky, "*Tinku, tinquichi* ... the place of the *encuentro*/encounter ... this is where you must come to reconcile all oppositions ... through Achuma to the

Land of the Achacillas ... come home to your beginnings which are the seeds of all our possible futures ..."

Words swirling through me.

The Aymara *Tinku* like the Hebrew *Tikun*, *Tikun Olam*, The Order of the World ... through the mind-opening road of the hallucinogenic cactus Achuma to the Land of the Achachillas, the Grandfathers/Ancestors ...

"This is the Sacred Centre, Nacan, Annaka, Nax, the centre, core, belly, bellybutton of the world ... you have come home to your beginnings, which are also all your possible futures ..."

The *ombligo*, umbilical centre of the world, Quiché Maya surging through me, the ancient pre-Columbian languages of Haiti and the Guayanas, fragments of ideas/words left behind by the ancient pilgrims on their way to the world-centre.

"*Chuki*, the Land of Gold, the gold-sky and golden land ..."

Chukiyawu, the original name for La Paz ... standing there, everything beginning to shine, all restored and clothed in gold again, the waters of the fountains flowing out of their artfully constructed basins, a waterfalling spout dropping into a basin that flowed underground again, emerging again into the sunlight, then underground, out, in, over and over again, the magic fountains described on the way to the Land of the Sun King in *The Odyssey*, which were really descriptions of the Sun King's Land itself, faintly remembered, passed down generation after generation, fragmentary memories of voyages from Anatolia to here, the world-mountain/world-centre, filtering into ancient Greece from a so much more ancient world in Asia Minor.

"*Pacha*, world, space, final judgement, *Taypi*, centre, *cola*, stone ..." the voices changing, condensing, only into *her* voice, "Now you shall become one with *Pachamama*, the great Earth as Mother, Mother of us All, you and I one with the earth that is one with the sky, at the moment of rebirth after temporary death ..."

I don't know how much Alexandra understood, could even 'hear' of the voices swirling around us. But I did feel she was inside the vision, standing there crying along with me ... seeing as I saw, everything differently, a puma carved into a wall, the image of the shamanic transformation I (we) had undergone.

Herakles again. The fanged god fanged because he had become divine.

Bird-snakes coming out of the top of his head, the uniting of sky (quetzal) and earth (coatl-snake) ... the Aztec *coatl* a combination of 'co' as in 'container' and 'atl,' water, so that all the fountained play of water here around us and in minds became a play of the Great Snake

Mother mating with Father Sky at this moment of maximum death and resurrection …

Everything 'spoke' to me.

The belly-button of the central figure on the sun-gate behind which the sun would rise the next morning on the day of the Winter Solstice. The calendrical-astronomical jaguar sun-god year-carrier from whose belly-button sprouted two more bird-fish, another fish twisted, lying on top of the central sun-symbol that I alone had seen for what it was, although it was the most obvious thing in the world, once you knew Indus Valley, Brahmi, Sumerian scripts:

The deltas (Δ) on the fish itself, doors opening into the infinite horizon of sacred apple-induced visions … the same motif repeated again and again, all over the giant stone statue called Kochamama:

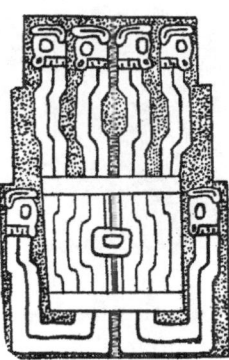

NAGA (Sanskrit), NAKU (Sumerian), NAKASH (Hebrew), NABA-ROA (Guarao), Nawach (Hopi) …

Water, water-serpents, the serpent in this, the original Garden of Eden, not evil as pictured in the bible, but the source of all fertility and joy.

This was my spiritual home and I understood every jaguar- and condor-head, every little Garudaish year-bearing bird:

He was Osiris, the sun-god man-bird:

The Assyrian god Assur crossing the sky in a winged disk:

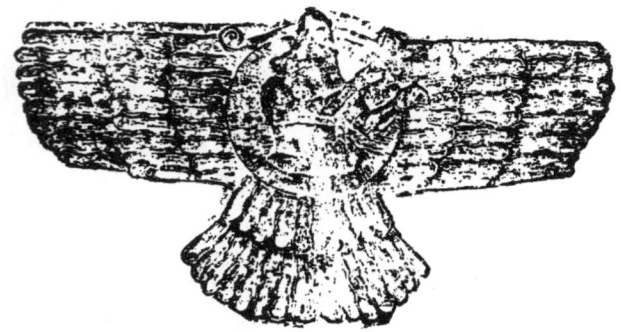

We wandered through the ruins for hours, time slowly running out for me, like sand through an hour glass. Alex knew what was coming.

She was almost as much a shaman as I, and when I turned to her toward the end of the day, about to say it was time for me to go on alone now, to the cave-world that had its entrance at the base of Mount Illimani, that she should wait for Ricardo and Maria del Carmen at the restaurant/refreshment stand where they said they would meet us, she already had read my thoughts and her answer was simply "Take me with you."

"No, you have all your life ahead of you, all I have is Past. It hardly makes any difference for me now, there is so little left. I am the prisoner of inevitability."

"You know how much I love you …"

"And how much I love you. Which is why I can't take you with me."

One last glance back at the old sun-god, Helios, carrying the two bird-snakes of the year in his hands.

I walked her back to the entrance, looked up overhead where the seven-headed serpent Losun/Ladon (Portuguese Latão-tin) would (what the Occident knew as the Pleiades) soon appear.

Of all my children, Alexandra in all her restlessness and creativity, intuitiveness, idealism, innocence, was the most like me.

"So what's going to happen to you?" she asked. "When will I see you again?"

"If I only knew …"

"Why are you doing this?"

"Do you believe that The Immortals have died?" I asked.

"Not really," she answered, sweeping the sad, despoiled ruins with her gaze, from horizon to horizon, scanning, imprinting it all on her soul, "they're still here in a way … almost erased … just traces left … but still here …"

"And you can hear what's out there, can't you?" I asked, turning toward Mount Illimani, the world-mountain, the original Intihuatana, The Place Where the Sun is Tied, every Inca ruin having a monolithic stone-post solstice-stone that was a pale, miniaturised replica of Mount Illimani itself.

She stood next to me facing Mount Illimani.

What I heard was a great roar, like a waterfall, pounding surf, jaguar growls, beckoning me. This was the night of the Descent into the Underworld, my personal Good (Bad) Friday when I would have to descend into Hell, die and be dismembered yet again. The year died; my own personal life replicated the cyclic birth-death rhythms of the stars.

I reached into my pocket and gave her all the money I had with me.

No last will, no testament. Everything was in order. She had her return ticket to the US, it was just a question of taking her to the airport. Most of the flights from Bolivia were half-empty anyhow, you never had to worry about reservations.

"So long, pal," I said, turned and started to walk in the direction of Thunder and Lightning Mountain.

I could hear her calling to me "Dad, Dad, Dad," but I didn't (couldn't) look back, just kept walking across the desolate landscape until I couldn't hear her any longer.

It was the end of scholarship for me now, little scholarly insights, links, correlations, dictionaries, walking into Sumerian and Akkadian, back through Tamil and Gond to proto-Dravidian, using Hebrew as a handy wrench to open up locked doors of the past. The end of museums, Cairo, Tunis, Mohenjo Daro, Harrapa, La Paz, Chicago. Visits to other sites that touched on, fed into this ultimate, final Home of the Gods – Ugarit, Çatak Hüyük, the rock reliefs at Yazilikaya, the lion gates at Hattusas that were faint echoes of their counterparts at Tiawanaku, Ur and Khafajeh, Ain Ghazal, Mari, Nimrud, Uruk, Babylon ...

The Taurus Mountains flowed through me now. I was drifting down the Euphrates past Akkad and Sumer, remembering the letter from Rib-Adda of Byblos to Amenophis IV, speaking of "The Great King ... my Lord ... the Sun-God ..."

I was there now, the Allpast flowing through me, cold, hungry (I should have taken some food with me, but, of course, I didn't), my heart beating twice its normal speed, wanting to just lie down and give up, wait for the Angel of Death to find me in the midst of all this rocky, dead desolation.

Too much wind, too much dust and dryness. And for every step I took forward it seemed like I had taken a step back, Illimani itself instead of growing larger as I advanced toward it, shrinking, diminishing down to nothingness.

The sun on the edge of the horizon now.

Ricardo and Maria del Carmen would have picked up Alex by now and they would have been all talking about what they should do. Should they come after me? Go to the police? Get help? Or just let me alone to my own devices and destiny?

Let me alone.

A shadow walking next to me now, with every step becoming a little more solid, at first amorphous and vague, but gradually assuming form, both our shadows at their ultimate lengthening now as the sun went down below the horizon, two jaguars/pumas, surrounded by our still-coalescing, form-taking peers, duplicating the rituals of prehistory, everyone coming now to the world-centre, every tribe, messenger, angel-demon, bird-soul, cat-soul, all the languages of the world flowing through me, Tiawanaku, Tiwatinaku, Torikaminotake, Mount Kunlun, the land of the Washu/Wanaku, Kahuna where Wanadi (Wanaku) the sun-god lives ...

A short dusk after sunset.

The vulture-king out of Guarajo myth was waiting for us, the sun-king with gilded human skins (Diodorus Siculus) in his closet, He Who Never Dies, living in the midst of the deathless, praying to myself "Vishnu, Vishnu, do not wake now and destroy us, we who are your dream."

Feeling more and more tenuous, cloudlike, unfleshed, my own jaguar-companion totally with me now as the moon rose and the landscape was platinised, silver-plated and we rolled together in the spirit-world like two spiralling tendrils of pure erotic energy.

She gave me some small fleshy 'buttons' to eat – which I ate, and the landscape became as red as blood and the two of us, my ageless lady and I swirled and swirled again together into orgasmic splicings of the purest joy.

Still walking, advancing on the mountain, surrounded by The Dead now, my father, not as I last saw him, heavy and sad, after his final heart attack, simply waiting to die, but young and idealistic, the gypsy violinist I had never known, my mother as I had never known her, daisy fields of exuberance, my dead brother, Noah, grown now, although he had died (meningitis) when he was only two, *abrazos, abrazos* and more *abrazos*, Phyllis Miller, who had been mutilated beyond recognition in a car crash when she was twenty-five, coming toward me restored and more than restored, "You know I always loved you," "And I you," Jackie Eubanks, funny and big and bouncy as always, wizened, philosopher-eyed Sidney Bernard and the great Kabbalist, my spiritual mentor, Menke Katz.

"I told you it would be this way!" he shouted, hands up like a referee calling a touchdown/goal, singing Shalom Aleichem the way he always sang it, only he himself an angel now, or a close (eternal) cousin ...

Then I looked again and they were all skulls, it was an army of skeletons marching toward the mouth of Hell, the landscape littered with bones, phantom vultures diving down and carrying bones away. Prometheus at night being devoured before his restoration the following dawn.

And who was I in the midst of all this drama of death and resurrection, crucified on the cross of my own ignorance and 'newness' to the game?

I was the voyager from across the sea, wasn't I, the one who had passed through the endless mind-zodiac puzzles of the last forty years of scholarship that everyone had said was wasted time ("No more books about Tiawanaku, please" – Al Silverstein, Prince of New York Agents), clashing gates and scorpio claws, lions and crabs and vultures, my whole life a tortured tumbling through the zodiac-vortex of the years ...

I was Prometheus, Odysseus, Herakles, Gilgamesh, Jason, Susanawo come at last to the World Mountain, Mashu, Meru, to die ... and be reborn ...

In Germanic myth Hel is the goddess who lives at the base of the world-mountain where Valhalla is on top, the Home of the Gods. And in German 'hel' is light, not darkness, like Helios the sun ...

HEL

HELIOS

So that the sun-king and the goddess of the underworld merge, the minotaur at the end of the (zodiac?) labyrinth, the sun-bull-man who emerges from Hell at the end/beginning of the solar year.

Where had Time gone to? I wondered as the sun (Hel/Helios) began to lighten the sky behind the World Mountain. Of course there was a resurrection. Of course there would be a New Covenant, a New Earth, a Second and a Third, an endless succession of Re-Comings. And the Holy Spirit wasn't just in us, but we were holy spirits ourselves now ... as the sun came up over Illimani and we approached the mouth of the cave beneath it, heard the flow of the holy river inside and saw the gold, bull-headed Yama – god of the Underworld – New Sun emerge and walk directly toward us ...

Editor's afterthoughts: The Immortals in British Myth

Within the myths and traditions of Britain and Ireland it's not difficult to find a number of resonances with the ideas put forward in *Immortal Jaguar*. When I mentioned these to Hugh he invited me to contribute a few notes; in doing so, I present them not so much as fixed and evidential connections but as seeds of thought and imagination.

In Britain and Ireland, the Immortals have their equivalent in the concept of Faery. The root tradition is strikingly similar: an ancient race of immortal beings with the gift of shape-shifting who at some time in the distant past withdrew from the outer world and retreated underground into the "hollow hills", where they still live, and can be contacted by mortal humans – though not without some peril for those who are ill-equipped to handle such encounters. In Ireland the myths are very well developed in a large range of stories and the Faery realm is called Tír Nan Óg: land of the ever-young. Immortality is given to those who enter Tír Nan Óg but on returning to the mortal world there is an instant catching up with the ageing process. Many people today are still able to come and go from Faery at will through shamanic visions, but there are also persistent myths from the past about those who were taken wholly and physically into Faery, and didn't always come back.

One such person was Thomas the Rhymer, or "True Thomas", who is the subject of a traditional Scottish folk song which amounts to a full scale initiatory ballad for those who look beyond its surface. It relates how Thomas is approached by the Queen of Faeries and after kissing or sleeping with her is taken into the world of Faery for a period of seven years. His journey with her takes him through a strange liminal netherworld where he sees neither sun nor moon (i.e. they are below ground) and rides through a river of blood where he can hear "the roaring of the sea". Eventually they come to the centre of the Underworld where a tree of apples or mixed fruits is growing. The Underworld Tree is a symbol found repeatedly in Celtic folklore, and its fruits are associated with magical transformation and visionary experience. Thomas plucks the fruit as a gift for the Faery Queen but she tells him not to eat them himself because they are poisonous to humans – in other words, they confer immortality, and once consumed he can never go back to ordinary human life.

On one level at least, Thomas the Rhymer was a real person. He was Lord Thomas Learmont of Erceldoune, a Scottish poet, political agitator and visionary of the 13th century. The small town of Erceldoune (now called Earlston) still bears a medieval ruin associated with him. Whether this prophet and faery-traveller was the originator of the ballad or simply became absorbed into an existing initiatory myth can only be speculated, but certainly the real-life Thomas was heavily associated with the "immortals" and in his own time was believed to have been taken bodily into the otherworld for a period of several years before returning to the human world with enhanced visionary powers.

Thomas' meeting with the Faery Queen also happened in a real place, the Eildon Hills in the lowlands of Scotland, which have legendary associations going back much earlier. They are traditionally believed to be hollow inside, and although this comes back to the "hollow hills" of Faery they are also reputed to contain a chamber or cavern in which the mythical King Arthur (in Britain we have a bear-king rather than a jaguar!) is sleeping along with his knights, awaiting the call to awaken and defend the land in time of need. There are many other places across the UK where King Arthur is supposed to be sleeping in underground caverns, and the persistence of this myth across multiple geographical locations shows a deep-rooted belief in an archetypal immortal king. The extant Arthurian legends describe how, when he was mortally wounded, Arthur was taken off to be healed in a land of immortals across the sea to the west. The name of this island is Avalon: Isle of Apples.

As in so many other cultures, the suggestion that the Americas had been reached by early mariners long before Columbus is a myth with deep roots in this part of the world.

Ireland has many legendary references to a land called Hy Brasil, the Isle of the Blessed, a phantom island in the west which was usually cloaked in mist and only became visible every seven years. This description of unchartable misty shores and seven year cycles places it firmly within the tradition of Faery. However there have also been speculations as to whether its origin is an encounter with the land of Brazil in ancient times. The mythical island appears on some maps as Brazil – though the name is derived from the Gaelic *Uí Breasail* (island of beauty, worth, mighty) and the name Brazil in South America is not from the same derivation, but it's still an interesting connection. It may be synonymous with the more recent legend of St Brendan's Island, another 'Isle of the Blessed' hidden by mist, which was visited by the Irish saint Brendan the Navigator in around 530 A.D. and led to much speculation as to whether St Brendan had actually reached the Americas some centuries before Columbus.

Rebecca Wilby